# Signs
## *of*
# His Presence

# Signs of His Presence

## Experiencing God's Comfort in Times of Suffering

Luann Mire *with* Patti Richter

Carpenter's Son Publishing

Signs of His Presence

©2019 by Luann Mire and Patti Richter

Published by Carpenter's Son Publishing, Franklin, Tennessee

Published in association with Larry Carpenter of Christian Book Services, LLC
www.christianbookservices.com

Scripture quotations, unless otherwise indicated, are taken from the Holy Bible, NEW INTERNATIONAL VERSION®, NIV® Copyright © 1973, 1978, 1984, 2011 by Biblica, Inc.® Used by permission. All rights reserved worldwide.

Scripture quotations marked (NLT) are taken from the Holy Bible, New Living Translation, copyright ©1996, 2004, 2015 by Tyndale House Foundation. Used by permission of Tyndale House Publishers, Inc., Carol Stream, Illinois 60188. All rights reserved.

Scripture quotations marked THE MESSAGE are taken from *THE MESSAGE,* copyright © 1993, 1994, 1995, 1996, 2000, 2001, 2002 by Eugene H. Peterson. Used by permission of NavPress. All rights reserved. Represented by Tyndale House Publishers, Inc.

Scripture quotations marked (ESV) are from The ESV® Bible (The Holy Bible, English Standard Version®), copyright © 2001 by Crossway, a publishing ministry of Good News Publishers. Used by permission. All rights reserved.

Scripture marked (NKJV) taken from the New King James Version®. Copyright © 1982 by Thomas Nelson. Used by permission. All rights reserved.

Some names have been changed to protect the privacy of individuals.

Edited by Robert Irvin

Cover and Interior Layout Design by Suzanne Lawing

Interior Illustrations by Andrew Mire

Printed in the United States of America

ISBN 978-1-946889-88-1

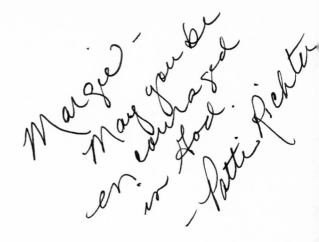

*. . . so that the work of God might be displayed.*

JOHN 9:3

**To Alan and Andrew**
*faithful and strong*

**To Alix and Kelsey**
*loving and kind*

**To Anna**
*joy upon joy*

*One generation will commend your works to another;*
*they will tell of your mighty acts.*

<small>PSALM 145:4</small>

# Foreword

*By Patti Richter*

In January 2011, I received an unexpected call from my friend Luann Mire in San Antonio. She sounded anxious, in a hurry. I could hardly fathom the words she was communicating: her husband, Pat, was facing a federal indictment related to a company where he formerly worked. She wanted me to know they desperately needed prayer.

I first met Luann the day my family moved into her neighborhood. Her cheerful presence at my door, along with a plate of cookies and her youngest son (the same age as my youngest son) kicked off an instant friendship. Though we had different church and school affiliations, our common faith and interest in ladies' Bible studies facilitated regular fellowship between us. For the ten years my family lived in the Alamo City, the Mires became more than good neighbors. They were friends we admired and trusted.

After my family moved to North Texas in 2007, my contact with Luann gradually became limited to holiday and birthday greetings, except for my infrequent visits. On those occasions, she and Pat provided me with their guest room and wonderful hospitality, even when my travel pertained to personal business.

Now, that January phone call was serving to hit the resume button on our friendship as I became a safe place for Luann to express concerns and seek prayer. We realized God had brought us together again for this time, and our reconnection eventually led to this book. As I sought to encourage my friend through her faith crisis brought by a legal nightmare, I marveled again and again over God's "ever-present help in trouble" (Psalm 46:1).

Helping Luann write her story—even as it was still unfolding—has strengthened my faith. I had to put all my chips on God's faithfulness to bring her family safely through the evil consequences of a justice system that can stack the deck against the innocent.

Like many of their friends, I've watched and waited for God to act on behalf of Luann and her family. I could not step into her shoes for the painful journey, but I could be her companion along the way. In *Signs of His Presence*, we've attempted to show what longsuffering can look like, and how God's encouragements are exceedingly greater than man's.

I hope this book will assure readers that God "is not far from each one of us" (Acts 17:28), and that he "is close to the brokenhearted and saves those who are crushed in spirit" (Psalm 34:18).

Those who trust in God yet suffer pain or loss can find a hopeful benediction in 1 Peter 5:10.

*And the God of all grace, who called you to his eternal glory in Christ, after you have suffered a little while, will himself restore you and make you strong, firm and steadfast.*

# Introduction

*Publish His glorious deeds.*

Psalm 96:3 (NLT)

"Do you renounce the spiritual forces of wickedness, and reject the evil powers of this world? Do you accept the freedom and power God gives you to resist evil, injustice, and oppression in whatever forms they present themselves?"[1]

I grew up accepting those questions as part of the profession of faith for my denomination, and I answered yes to them without much thought. But the day would come when those questions would become extremely personal to me. I would need to reckon with those inherent truths and seek the power God provides to withstand evil.

Until a few years ago, my faith journey did not include an awareness of evil or Satan's schemes. I somehow only glanced at the Bible's references to the powers of darkness, which—to my knowledge—had never before troubled me.

I grew up in a happy Christian home, cherished by my parents, who had been married ten years before my birth. For two years their world revolved around me before their orbit expanded with the arrival of my sister, Beth.

The local Methodist church served as the center of our family activities. Dad taught Sunday school, including my class for several years. I followed my parents' model of serving by playing the piano for Sunday worship during high school.

I kept up with church attendance through college, and that commitment grew after I began dating Pat Mire, who would become my husband. (He grew up Catholic, so missing church was not an option.) After we married, we joined a Methodist church and eventually taught Sunday school together and sponsored youth retreats.

We spent two years in New Orleans and another in Memphis, and our family grew to include two sons, Alan and Andrew, who were born three years apart. In both places, we dove into church life and were involved in several areas. And when Pat's job brought us to San Antonio, we searched for a church before buying a house. We also decided that I would stay at home to keep everything afloat. I felt privileged to give myself fully to family, friends, and church.

We truly sensed the Holy Spirit moving in our new church, and, again, I poured myself into several ministries. My areas of service changed throughout the various seasons of my life, but never ceased. I believed that being a good Christian meant "doing."

In my late thirties, after the boys began school, I worked part-time. Though my passion remained focused on my family, I also developed a greater desire to spend quiet time with God and in His Word each day. I felt as if Jesus' words to Martha applied to me: "Luann, Luann, you are worried and upset about many things, but only one thing is needed." My morning devotion time grew until I began to feel cheated if I didn't have an hour in God's presence. But, somehow, I found a way to turn my habit of prayer into a monthly duty by offering to teach a class for new church members on the topic of spending time alone with God.

I gradually became a prayer warrior through the practice of journaling my prayers by filling notebooks with the joys and sorrows of my faith journey. For years I never realized how vital this habit would be to my spiritual health. In the beginning of this closer walk with God, I feared getting too close to Him. Maybe He would think I could handle a tragedy. And, with more attention to Scripture, I saw how Satan attacks the servants of God.

Spiritual warfare became real to me. Ephesians 6:12 says: "For our struggle is not against flesh and blood, but against the rulers, against the authorities, against the powers of this dark world and against the spiritual forces of evil in the heavenly realms." I learned to fight daily in my "prayer chair" while claiming God's promises. I understood with new clarity the words of 1 John 3:8: "The reason the Son of God appeared was to destroy the devil's work."

My faith tradition included a third question for membership: "Do you confess Jesus Christ as your Savior, put your whole trust in his grace, and promise to serve him as your Lord?"[2]

I wholeheartedly answered yes and have always tried to serve God. Even so, when I sensed His urging me to write this story, I told Him it would be too painful. He answered with gentle encouragement, reminding me of His promise: "'Because he loves me,' says the Lord, 'I will rescue him; I will protect him, for he acknowledges my name. He will call upon me, and I will answer him; I will be with him in trouble, I will deliver him and honor him'" (Psalm 91:14, 15).

Despite what my family has endured, it now seems a privilege to tell this story of God's compassionate love.

—*Luann Mire*

# See Clearly

*God gives us sight for seeing;*
*He leads us toward the light.*
*In the beauty He's created,*
*We view our future bright.*

*But should we trust our eyes?*
*Distractions are Satan's key.*
*Our faith in God is stronger*
*When we believe and do not see.*

*Now let His true light guide you*
*And know that He is near—*
*For though this world grows darker,*
*He makes your vision clear.*

*So, close your eyes, believers,*
*Open your hearts and mind.*
*You'll bask in all His glory*
*And know that He's divine.*

—PAT MIRE

# Contents

# Chapter 1

# Ties That Bind

*. . . so the Lord surrounds his people.*
Psalm 125:2

Cooking pot roast absorbed my attention one blustery January afternoon. After chopping onions and slicing carrots, I set the table for seven couples.

My husband, Pat, and I had offered to host our weekly Bible study due to another couple's conflicting schedule. As I worked in the kitchen, I heard a loud thumping noise overhead that sent me outside to investigate.

From the front porch, I looked up through the oak trees and saw a blue helicopter—hovering so close that I felt vibrations as its blades cut the air above me. I wondered what could be happening in the neighborhood on a Monday. Even so, with guests arriving soon, I turned back—just in time to hear the house phone ringing.

I hurried toward the kitchen, anxious to hear from Pat. He

had called earlier in the day to let me know he needed to go downtown to the courthouse at the request of a federal prosecutor.

When I answered the phone, I heard a quiver in my husband's voice. "Luann, they are indicting me—just me—on twenty-nine counts."

"Pat! I don't understand! How could they indict you? You were completely unaware. How can this be?"

My heart raced as our panicked conversation ended. I called one of our guests and asked if she would come early. I needed help!

Pat came home—shaking, crying—about the same time that our friends began to arrive. Everyone appeared bewildered as they heard about the indictment, and they shared our distress.

Somehow, we ate dinner. But afterward, instead of our regular study, we all prayed and kept praying. Afterward, our prayer leader, Mark, asked us to open our Bibles to Psalm 91. Pat and I bowed our heads as Mark began to read this prayer of protection.

> He who dwells in the shelter of the Most High will rest in the shadow of the Almighty. I will say of the Lord, "He is my refuge and my fortress, my God in whom I trust." Surely he will save you from the fowler's snare (Psalm 91:1-3).

After everyone left, our friends Mitch and Shelly knocked at the front door. They wanted to prepare us for what they had just seen: A local television news report showed an aerial view—helicopter footage—of our home.

We faced the fight of our lives.

22

Pat and I made San Antonio our home when our sons, Alan and Andrew, were young. The city was centrally located to our extended family, and we grew attached to our local Methodist church. But, in order to avoid a move, Pat needed to consider a job change because his company required regular transfers for senior executives.

Pat found another sales position with a locally based company, and within two years another opportunity presented itself. This new role as sales manager for a professional employment organization seemed perfect for Pat. And the job offered an added bonus for our family since his new employer, Carl, and his wife shared our faith. This couple frequently welcomed us into their home for fellowship, singing, and prayer with their church friends.

Our lives progressed in a happy blur of family and church activities. Through the years, Pat and I enjoyed teaching our sons' Sunday school classes and chaperoning their youth retreats and summer mission trips. Pat also helped coach Alan's and Andrew's various teams—soccer, baseball, basketball, and football.

Dark clouds began to gather around us beginning with the loss of Pat's father, "Poppy," whose number one goal in life was to make others happy. We lost him to cancer when he was only 65.

Further concerns developed as Pat felt increasingly isolated by Carl concerning management decisions. After several years of working for him, Pat started his own employment service company. My husband's business flourished in an environment of mutual trust between Pat, his employees, and his clients.

Four years after Pat severed his employment under Carl, we heard news that made us especially thankful for that decision.

Pat's former coworkers informed him that Carl faced serious legal problems due to unpaid taxes going back more than ten years—long before we knew him.

At this time, Pat called the FBI on his own; his purpose was to request a meeting. He wanted to know why they were questioning his clients regarding Carl's tax activities. When he arrived at the meeting, however, a federal prosecutor was present. Pat had no legal representation since he never imagined he had any cause for concern.

My own concerns during this time revolved around the failing health of my parents and the subsequent loss of my childhood home in Deer Park, near Houston. Due to my mother's signs of Alzheimer's disease and my father's congestive heart failure, they decided to move closer to my sister, Beth, in East Texas, where my parents had lived in their early years of marriage. While Beth's proximity to our parents eased my worries, the change meant twice the driving distance for me—six hours instead of three.

Changes at our beloved church caused additional apprehension for Pat and me.

Alan had graduated from high school, but as Andrew approached his senior year, the once-vibrant youth ministry now stood on shaky ground. With several staff departures, the church needed to hire a new youth director.

Pat and I offered to teach eleventh- and twelfth-grade Sunday school and recruited other couples to help, even though we had no curriculum. We already hosted Andrew's high school boys' Bible study in our home every Wednesday night, which we had done for the past four years. However, we dug in to help our church maintain its Sunday outreach to youth.

While many of our church friends left to seek another place

of worship, I held the ingrained conviction that your congregation is your family; you do not just leave it. Pat and I lamented the continuing loss of fellowship. This overall concern for the direction of our church caused many sleepless nights for me.

Now, with this just-announced indictment, the dark clouds intensified. We were blindsided.

The day after the helicopter invasion, Alan and Andrew, now together in college at Texas A&M, drove home from College Station to be with us. Pat's mother, Linda, and his brother Rod, along with a close family friend, also arrived from the Houston area.

We all sat at the kitchen table; there was no thought of eating. The morning newspaper featured an article with a photo of Pat in handcuffs, which happened when he first arrived at the courthouse the previous day. The prosecutor had conveniently arranged a "photo op" to announce the indictment to the media. After that short-lived moment ended, the deputy in charge of the cuffs apologized to Pat, saying he had only followed protocol.

My sons tried to shield me from reading the article, but I couldn't help seeing that photo. The image distressed me so much I could barely breathe. This sudden attack on Pat's character traumatized all of us. How could this be happening to him instead of Carl—the one responsible for any criminal activity!

On Wednesday, after everyone left, Pat and I met several friends for an evening communion service at church. The sermon topic, "I'm Taking It," reminded us that Jesus is our burden bearer. But our crushing burden rendered me too distraught to feel God's presence.

The next morning Pat went to his weekly men's Bible study. His friend Perry, unaware of the psalm Mark had read over us Monday evening, handed Pat a copy of the same psalm. Perry's wife, Dee Dee, had inserted Pat's name into the prayerful verses of Psalm 91.

That afternoon, Pat and I met with a former associate pastor from our church. While we sat in her new office, she invited another staff member to join us in prayer. This man, a stranger to us, began to recite Psalm 91, praying the verses over us by memory, word for word.

This repetition of Scripture—three times in three days from three different sources—gave me an assurance of God holding my hand. Though I couldn't understand what was happening, I knew He was with us.

When Mark and his wife, Lynn, had us over for dinner that Friday night, he remarked, "I can't wait to see the stories God is going to unfold with this ordeal."

And the ordeal began to unfold with a bit of clarity later that same night, when I had difficulty sleeping.

While Pat whimpered in his sleep, I sat up in bed, pained to hear him doing so. Fully awake and wondering if I should wake him, I saw a bright red light near the ceiling in the far corner of our room. Gripped with fear, I sensed the presence of evil, and I whispered, "Jesus. Jesus. Jesus. In the name of Jesus Christ, I rebuke you." In my spirit, I heard a clear and haunting reply: *My name is Bar-Jesus.* Only one thought went through my head.

*Bar-Jesus!* Who *is Bar-Jesus?*

# Chapter 2

# Reassurance and Revelation

*You will not fear the terror of night,*
*nor the arrow that flies by day.*

Psalm 91:5

I slipped out of bed long before daylight, not fearful, but determined to find out anything about Bar-Jesus. Reaching for my thick robe, I headed to the solitude of the den and curled up in the overstuffed chair by our fireplace—my prayer chair. In the Bible dictionary on the chairside table, I found a reference to Bar-Jesus that directed me to Acts 13:6-10.

> There they met a Jewish sorcerer and false prophet named Bar-Jesus, who was an attendant of the proconsul, Sergius Paulus. The proconsul, an intelligent man, sent for Barnabas and Saul because he wanted to hear the word of God. But Elymas the sorcerer (for that is what his name means) opposed them and tried to turn

the proconsul from the faith. Then Saul, who was also called Paul, filled with the Holy Spirit, looked straight at Elymas and said, "You are a child of the devil and an enemy of everything that is right! You are full of all kinds of deceit and trickery. Will you never stop perverting the right ways of the Lord?"

This passage was unfamiliar to me; if someone had asked me about Bar-Jesus the day before, I would have been clueless. Did Paul's rebuke to that man apply to our circumstances? Was God showing me that our battle was against evil forces?

When Pat came to breakfast later, he listened with relative calm as I told him about my vision during the night. Like me, he didn't know what to think about this revelation. We both felt confused about how to proceed.

Though Pat had secured a lawyer, several friends urged us to find additional legal representation. We contacted an attorney friend from church, and he invited us to his home for lunch that same day. While Pat carried his thick indictment packet to the car, I brought along my Bible.

As we sat with Larry and his wife, Margie, at their kitchen table, I pointed to the indictment and said, "We were attacked with this situation." Then, pointing to the Bible, I added, "And now we have this Bar-Jesus situation."

The couple validated our concern regarding both the legal and spiritual attack against us, then prayed with us. They also encouraged Pat, as the head of our family and my spiritual "covering," to specifically pray over me each night before bed.

Margie suggested we have our home anointed with prayer. She offered to call a mutual friend of ours, Marthe, about meeting at our house. Pat and I didn't understand what this involved, but we trusted these longtime friends.

After Sunday worship the next day—six days after the

indictment—we met Pat's brother and sister-in-law, Kenny and Wendye, who drove in from Austin. During our lunch together, Margie called to say they could come by our house that afternoon. This necessitated telling Kenny and Wendye about Bar-Jesus. Though I was reluctant to talk about the strange encounter, I felt relieved after sharing my story with family.

Margie and Marthe arrived with a small vial of oil, which symbolized the presence and power of the Holy Spirit. The six of us passed it around to anoint one another's hands and forehead. As we proceeded to pray in each room of our home, Pat received a call from an attorney recommended to us by a close friend. The timing of this call—coming as we prayed—seemed significant later, when we chose this man's firm to represent Pat.

I knew we faced a supernatural foe, but I also knew we had a supernatural commander, One who says, "Do not be afraid or discouraged because of this vast army. For the battle is not yours, but God's" (2 Chronicles 20:15).

On the tenth day after the indictment, I awoke from a dream where I was fighting evil by singing praise songs. That same morning, I drove a few streets over to my monthly neighborhood prayer meeting. Aware of my circumstances, a woman in our group expressed her belief that praising God was the only way to fight the evil. She began to sing, and we all joined her in the familiar song taken from Psalm 18: *Praise the name of Jesus; praise the name of Jesus. He's my rock, He's my fortress, He's my deliverer; in Him do I trust.*

That evening, two other friends, unconnected to each other

or to that particular prayer group, each sent me a text that included 2 Samuel 22:2, 3 which says: "The Lord is my rock, my fortress and my deliverer; my God is my rock, in whom I take refuge." These words in David's song of deliverance from his enemies are also recorded in Psalm 18. And now they were repeated to me—three times in one day!

This repetition gave me chills. I believed God used His Word to assure me of His help.

I claimed that Scripture song as our battle cry and learned to play it on the piano. Even when I felt like crying instead of singing praise songs, I would sing this one to my heavenly commander.

During this time I had been too rattled to venture out alone. But after two weeks without driving, I finally headed to a nearby Christian bookstore to look for the birthday gift I had in mind for Wendye. I went straight to the Bible section and knelt in front of the shelves.

"Can I help you?" A tall salesman looked down at me.

"I'm fine," I said. "I'm here to get a *Life Application Bible* in the NIV."

"Psalm 27:8 tells us to seek His face," the man said.

I paused and looked up at this gentleman, who looked about the age of my dad. He had just said exactly what I told my mother-in-law when everything first hit us. I had explained to Linda that if I could feel God's presence and see Him working in our situation, I would have peace.

The salesman reached for a copy of a paraphrased version of the Bible. "I really like the way Eugene Peterson writes in *The Message*," he said.

"Yes, I like that version. But I want the *Life Application Bible* for my sister-in-law," I said, smiling.

"But I just love the way Peterson writes." Clearly, this man was persistent. "Chapter nine of John comforts me concerning our three grandchildren born with the same disease. They all died before age three." He opened *The Message* and began reading:

> Walking down the street, Jesus saw a man blind from birth. His disciples asked, "Rabbi, who sinned: this man or his parents, causing him to be born blind?"
>
> Jesus said, "You're asking the wrong question. You're looking for someone to blame. There is no such cause-effect here. Look instead for what God can do. We need to be energetically at work for the One who sent me here, working while the sun shines."[1]

After hearing that passage, I sat down—right there on the floor. I'd been asking myself that very question again and again. Who is to blame, and why would this indictment happen to my husband, an innocent man? It struck me, right there, and I realized that John chapter nine teaches that all is done for the glory of God.

While the salesman—his name tag said Larry—took a phone call, I pondered these things and tried to focus on choosing a Bible color. When he returned, he began to tell me more about his family.

"I have four children," Larry said, "and I have to tell you that my wife and I were very worried about our youngest son, Andrew."

Hearing the name Andrew, I almost felt sick. I worried about our Andrew; I knew the temptations he faced as a college freshman.

The kind salesman went on. "God told me that only He could save Andrew," Larry said. "And He did. Today, Andrew is 45 years old with children of his own. He's a successful man who walks with the Lord."

I stood up—wobbly-kneed—convinced that God was speaking to me through this man.

After the salesman inquired about my church and recognized the name, he mentioned that his grandson served as part of the worship team for the contemporary service, and I recognized the young man's name.

"I really admired your former pastor," he added.

Larry proceeded to tell me about a start-up church "with solid teaching" that he and his wife were attending. He didn't realize Pat and I had recently visited the same church!

By now this man had addressed four things that had plagued my mind for weeks: trying to see God's presence in our circumstances, wondering who to blame, worrying about Andrew, and stressing over concerns for our church. Before I checked out, he recommended a book for men, saying, "As a young man, I was not a good husband, not very thoughtful."

This gave me a chance to tell him about Pat. "I have a wonderful husband who makes the bed and coffee every morning. He cares for me tenderly, always putting my needs before his own."

"Your husband sounds simply perfect," Larry said.

"My husband is perfect."

I left the bookstore believing I'd had a divine appointment with this salesman. Larry served as my "Jesus-with-skin-on" that day.

In the past two weeks, I had encountered both Bar-Jesus and my Jesus-with-skin-on. Though I thanked God for providing daily insight and encouragement, I still faced recurring anxiety. This state of mind was so foreign to me that it made me wonder if I was under spiritual attack. When I mentioned this to a friend, she recommended that I read E.M. Bounds' classic work, *Guide to Spiritual Warfare.*

Completely absorbed with the Bounds book, I shared some passages with Pat one day as we drove to a grocery store. In response, he gave me an offhand, casual reply. "I don't care about the devil," Pat said, "and I'm not afraid of him."

I gently reminded Pat of a warning from 2 Peter 2:11 that even angels do not dare dispute with the devil. "We can't underestimate Satan's power," I added.

That topic of conversation ended until we finished shopping and began driving home. Back on the busy four-lane road, Pat slammed on the brakes and stopped the car in the middle of traffic.

"Luann, I can't see at all! Everything is dark."

"What's wrong with you?" I shouted.

Not knowing what to do, I grabbed the wheel.

"I just went blind! I had to stop."

Within a minute, Pat's vision returned to normal, and he began driving again.

"That was so strange," he said a few minutes later. "Do you realize I went blind in the exact same spot where I said I wasn't afraid of the devil?"

That strange incident marked our newly shared conviction: Satan's forces are in our midst whether we want to believe it or not. And we knew we could only navigate these uncharted waters through continual prayer and reliance on God's Word.

In 1 John 3:8, the apostle John wrote, "The reason the

Son of God appeared was to destroy the devil's work." The commentary in my Bible explains: "Many in our world today mock the supernatural. They deny the reality of the spiritual world. . . . Don't take Satan and his supernatural powers of evil lightly, and don't become arrogant about how defeated he will be. Although Satan will be destroyed completely, he is at work now trying to render Christians complacent and ineffective."[2]

A book on spiritual warfare, *Beautiful Battle,* by Mary DeMuth, provided further insight for me. The author asserts:

> Having a high view of God and a proper theology of Satan helps us live victoriously, not overly scared of Satan's traps, but living in proper fear of a holy, powerful God who loves us and has already secured our deliverance.[3]

The first epistle of John says, "You, dear children, are from God and have overcome [evil spirits], because the one who is in you is greater than the one who is in the world" (1 John 4:4).

Another Scripture also assures us, "The Lord will rescue me from every evil attack and will bring me safely to his heavenly kingdom" (2 Timothy 4:18).

Pat and I actually took comfort in acknowledging the forces of evil in this world. Because we had seen the supernatural evidence of evil, we could likewise anticipate seeing the goodness of our supernatural God.

# Chapter 3

# Strength for the Distance

*I will fear no evil, for you are with me.*
PSALM 23:4

My parents lived in their new home near Beth's family in Henderson for two years with the help of caregivers. But the day came when Mom needed to be moved into a twenty-four-hour care facility.

Pat and I made the six-hour drive to help with my mother's transition. We stayed with Dad for several days before leaving for College Station; Alan's graduation from Texas A&M fell on Saturday of this same week.

At the ceremony, I tried to enjoy our son's milestone and appreciate his achievements, but I could not stop crying during what should have been a celebration. My heart was still with my mother.

After just two weeks in the nursing facility, Mom developed a severe kidney infection and had to be moved to a hospital in

Tyler. Beth called to say I should come right away.

As I packed my car, a red cardinal perched on the iron fence by our driveway. The bird waited as if he wanted me to acknowledge his presence. I thought, *God, are you telling me that you are with me in this grief?* The nearness of the bird gave me encouragement and peace even while I was shaking at my core.

Mother's kidney infection signaled the beginning of her organs shutting down. Beth and I made arrangements to move Mom to a hospice facility that was also in Tyler. We grieved at the finality of this decision but felt relief to see Mom free of pain in times of consciousness.

Dad couldn't bear to see Mom failing, so Beth and I took turns staying with them—one of us at Dad's house and the other with Mom. The hospice vigil was difficult and lonely. I made frequent trips outside to the facility patio to make and receive calls from family and friends. Each time, a single cardinal came near, landing on a limb or the ground. These striking visitations reinforced the strong sense that God was with me. I had to let go of Mom, but God would not let go of me.

Days turned to weeks while Mother lingered, yet the cardinals lingered too, everywhere I went. I saw one each morning at Beth's house before making the hour-long drive to Tyler. And in my stays with Dad, I saw them in his yard. The cardinals comforted and cheered me as friends might do if they could surround me.

On one of those days, I had more than a feathered friend when Patti Richter drove from her home in Dallas—90 miles away. We'd been both neighbors and good friends for the ten years she lived in San Antonio. Patti's willingness to visit me in Tyler meant so much during my isolation in a strange city where I didn't know anyone. Seeing her lifted my spirits and allowed me to share the phenomenon of the cardinals, which astonished her. She also visited my sweet mother and joined me in prayer for God's perfect timing concerning Mom's departure.

In those two weeks of quiet waiting, I reflected on the blessing of having a mother who nurtured her family and others, including many students over her years of teaching. Mother also gracefully tended to her home until her illness disrupted the last few years.

My parents had been married sixty years. I wondered how Dad would live without Mom. It saddened me that he couldn't bear to visit her at the hospice facility. But then God intervened.

As I sat in Mom's room one afternoon with the door opened, I noticed a woman in the hallway who I instantly recognized—one of my favorite middle school teachers! Mrs. Baty was my seventh- and eighth-grade English teacher in Deer Park, almost 250 miles from Tyler.

Mrs. Baty peeked in and recognized me as well. "Are you Luann?" Her surprise equaled mine. "My husband has just been placed in the next room."

My former teacher's familiar face and kind inquiries about my mom and dad comforted me. I recalled how she once encouraged me to hone my writing skills. She nurtured both my mind and my confidence as a student.

When I relayed the news of our hospice neighbors to Dad, he said, "I need to go see your mom and Mrs. Baty."

Pat drove to be with me each weekend. One Saturday, he picked up Dad in Henderson and brought him to Tyler. Dad could barely manage to enter the room where Mom lay unresponsive, but at least he could see that she was peaceful.

Just one week later, Mother left us.

I spent Mom's final days by her side with quiet hymns playing. I silently praised God for the mother He had given me and His presence with us during this time.

Pat and the boys arrived the morning after Mom passed away. As we gathered around Dad at my parents' home, Pat noticed something: a ceramic cardinal sat on top of their bookshelf. I had been too preoccupied to notice the figurine she had kept from the time of my childhood. I saw it now with fresh eyes.

Many of our family members and friends made the long drive to be with us for the funeral, and this provided much comfort. And God provided one final consolation for this solemn day. As I turned to leave the cemetery, a male cardinal swooped down to the fresh dirt beside Mother's grave. The redbird paused just long enough for me to notice him. Then he flew away.

As our summer resumed, I found solace at the lake house we bought when the boys were still in grade school. Pat and I had enjoyed bringing the run-down cottage back to life. The country place with one bedroom and a converted porch that served as a second bedroom was only an hour from our home. The property had become a quiet haven for our family and friends to celebrate life together. We served many meals prepared in the low-ceilinged kitchen, and we provided wall-to-wall sleeping accommodations in the small den with its pine floors and limestone fireplace.

The lake house provided a place for me to reflect on Mother's life and grieve her death. Yet we also now began having frequent uninvited house guests: the local squirrels shredded toilet paper in the bathroom drawers and stashed acorns behind the sofa cushions. They had found crevices for their nests between our visits!

Further, we discovered all of the support beams were rotten. Though we had shored up the old house with earlier renovations, it was evident we needed to do something drastic. The house—like everything else in our life right now—was at risk of crumbling around us. Not only would we need to repair the sixty-year-old foundation, we would also need to address the walls, ceiling, roof, flooring, windows, doors, plumbing, and electrical.

We decided to rebuild using the same floor plan with a few improvements. We plunged ahead, gutting the house down to the concrete slab. The reconstruction project proved therapeutic for Pat and me. Tearing down walls and filling trash containers diverted our thoughts from the legal proceedings, which had paralyzed us since that fateful day in January.

One friend likened the death and resurrection of the house to our lives. "It unexpectedly gets scraped bare to its foundation," she said. "Now it will be filled with good things for the life of your family."

Pat and I both enjoy home remodeling; it has been a shared hobby for thirty years. I savor the creative aspect while Pat embraces the challenge of the carpentry work. In this way, and in every way, we make a compatible working team. When an idea hits me, Pat figures out a way to make it work.

The renovated house didn't compare to the old one; it was stronger and better in every way. A resurrection indeed.

While we stayed busy with our building project that summer, both of our boys worked with Christian ministries. Alan served as director of counselors at Laity Lodge Youth Camp in the Texas Hill Country. Andrew spent half the summer working as a counselor at the same camp. Then he worked with Perry and Dee Dee at Blueprint Ministries, an organization they founded to repair substandard housing in San Antonio.

Pat continued meeting with both his attorneys and the prosecutor, who insisted that Pat must plead guilty to some involvement. However, as a victim of his employer's illegal activity, Pat rejected the prosecutor's implication of guilt. He knew he couldn't plead guilty to a crime he didn't commit.

In mid-August we took a family vacation. Alan would soon move to Austin to begin his career as a CPA, and Andrew would return to A&M to begin his sophomore year. The trip gave us five days together in the cool climate of Idaho. We felt blessed to escape the oppressive Texas heat and the equally overbearing legal circumstances.

After returning from the relaxing getaway, Pat and I helped Alan with his move and then turned around to take furniture to College Station for Andrew's new A&M living quarters. Although I felt exhausted after moving furniture and unloading boxes in 100-degree-plus heat, it was "a good tired."

We were thrilled about Alan's new job and excited about Andrew's new house and roommates—all were Christian young men.

We desperately wanted life to have a sense of peace and normalcy. But another season of pain was about to hit us.

I talked to Dad at least once every day, as usual, but I knew something was wrong when he called late one evening after we'd already talked twice that day.

"Luann, I don't know all the details, but Beth has been burned, and Clay said she's being transported to Dallas by helicopter."

"What happened?" I tried to suppress my fear.

"I'm not sure. Clay said something about their outdoor grill flaring up."

When we hung up, I immediately called my brother-in-law, Clay, who explained that weather delayed the helicopter. Instead, Beth was taken by ambulance to a Dallas burn center.

Just three months after losing my mom, I couldn't bear the thought of losing Beth too. By morning, I was able to talk with her and felt relief to hear the limited extent of her injuries. While she suffered burns to her right arm, hand, and both legs, the doctor assured her of a full recovery in the next several months. She would be released later that day.

Though Beth had dodged a bullet, this accident made me uneasy. The timing of her injury may have been coincidental, but I connected it to the evil assault against us.

The same day Beth returned home, Pat met with his attorneys and learned the federal prosecutor was continuing to demand a guilty plea from Pat to strengthen his case against Carl. We were in disbelief. Yet we kept in mind the revelation of Bar-Jesus. We had to wonder if this is how evil operates. How could Pat plead guilty to a crime he'd known nothing about until years later? We could only pray: "God, please show us what to do. Should we trust the attorneys we believe You placed in our lives?"

Later that same evening, our ten-year-old dog, Spencer, would not lift his head. We took him to an emergency veterinary clinic and left him for observation but checked on him several times over the weekend. After church on Sunday, we waited to see Spencer in the yard of the clinic. When we called to him, a single red cardinal perched on the fence next to us; its sudden arrival immediately provided comfort.

On Monday morning, however, the vet explained that Spencer was covered with malignant tumors. He recommended putting him to sleep! How could this be? We hadn't even realized he was sick. That same afternoon, Pat and I cried and consoled each other as we said goodbye to our beloved pet.

The unexpected loss of Spencer, combined with Mother's recent passing, the prosecutor's relentless tactics, and Beth's burns, gave us too much to process. But this season of sorrows would only intensify, beginning two days later.

On Wednesday, Beth called to say that Dad went by ambulance to the Tyler hospital after his defibrillator activated, causing him to fall in his garage.

Pat and I left for Tyler early the next morning and stayed several days until Dad was cleared to go home. Since Beth still needed to recover from her burns, our aunt and uncle came to stay with Dad so Pat and I could return to San Antonio. And the caregiver who had attended Mother now came each day to help Dad.

By now I was shaken, even fearful. Too much was happening at once. Had Satan's forces targeted us like God's servant Job? I poured out my painful woes to God in my journal, asking Him to thwart the enemy's plans and send His mighty angels to deliver us from any evil.

Sylvia Gunter's book, *Blessing Your Spirit*, offered insight that addressed my fears: "The enemy will do everything possible to magnify the pain and cause you to focus on the pain . . . "[1]

Pat and I planned to visit Dad the following week and take him to a school reunion where he would be honored as a former teacher. I had a strong feeling I should miss the women's Bible study I taught on Thursday mornings so we could have more time with Dad.

We arrived early enough that day to take Dad to Beth's house for dinner in the evening. Although Mom was gone, it was wonderful to be together again.

Later, during the night at Dad's house, I heard him coughing and checked on him several times. He assured me he was fine, but at breakfast he seemed agitated—not himself. After the caregiver arrived for the day, Beth and I left for an appointment to sign papers for our mother's estate. Pat was happy to stay with Dad.

While we were out, Dad's caregiver called to say we should come home right away. We returned within five minutes, but it was too late.

Dad had died of a massive heart attack.

In this unexpected new grief, I could be grateful for at least two things. We had arrived early enough to spend the previous day with Dad. And Pat was there with Dad in the last moments of his life.

On the morning of the funeral a few days later, I read through the book of James—my dad's name. "Blessed is the man who perseveres under trial, because when he has stood the test, he will receive the crown of life that God has promised to those who love him" (James 1:12).

Dad had been a man of few words. He exemplified James 1:19: "Everyone should be quick to listen, slow to speak and slow to become angry." Another verse, James 3:13, spoke to me of Dad's character: "Who is wise and understanding among you? Let him show it by his good life, by deeds done in the humility that comes from wisdom."

We buried Dad next to Mom. And since her gravestone hadn't been made yet, we ordered one that included both their names. I took comfort in knowing my parents were together. Dad would not have to endure any holidays or birthdays without her. They would celebrate together with Jesus.

As I got in the car to leave Dad's grave, a familiar friend came to console me: a single red cardinal flew by. Though I longed for my earthly father, I could see—in living color—that my heavenly Father would never leave me.

Back home five days later, I woke with the words of our battle cry in my spirit: "Praise the name of Jesus. He's my rock. He's my fortress. He's my deliverer; in Him will I trust." While my soul grieved and my mind couldn't comprehend anything that was happening in my life at this time, my spirit could still praise God.

Trying to resume my normal routine that morning, I poured a cup of coffee and sat down to pen my prayer in a journal, asking God to make me mentally, spiritually, and physically whole again.

A chirping sound interrupted my devotional time. Do cardinals chirp? I didn't know. Hoping for one more reminder of God's presence, I got up to open the shutter. A single red cardinal appeared to be calling me as he perched on a sprinkler head in the yard.

I cried in amazement at a God who could answer my

doubts and console my spirit. The words of Job 19:25 rushed from my lips: "I know that my Redeemer lives . . . "

My fiftieth birthday arrived ten days after my father's death. Close friends gathered around me again, and this gave me a glimpse of Heaven. I could enjoy the company of those who loved the Lord and loved me! Considering the past nine months—beginning with the indictments—I hoped this milestone would signal the end of sorrows and a better season of life.

Instead, it would prove to be a marker on a much longer journey.

Evil seemed to shadow us as we dealt with legal maneuvers. The prosecutor insisted on using Pat to convict his former employer. He threatened Pat with going to trial on all twenty-nine counts if he refused to plead guilty in some way. And the prosecutor added that he wouldn't indict Carl at all unless Pat agreed to this plan. We felt especially bullied after being told the government could go after me as well since I had worked part-time for Pat.

Pat's attorney assured him that pleading guilty on just two of the counts would only connect him to having worked for Carl and would differentiate him from any direct involvement in their fraudulent schemes. Pat also would have the opportunity to tell his story to the judge, his attorney said. Since Pat wanted Carl convicted so we could resume our lives without this legal cloud hanging over us, he reluctantly—and with much apprehension—acquiesced to the attorney's plan.

First, the prosecutor insisted Pat plead guilty to mail fraud because insufficient insurance certificates had been mailed through the U.S. postal system when Pat worked for Carl. However, Pat had been completely unaware of any misrepresentation at that time since Carl assured him all their insurance had the proper underwriting. This important fact did not matter to the prosecutor.

The prosecutor also demanded a guilty plea for money laundering. Pat had loaned money from his personal account to Carl's company at a prominent local bank's request for necessary payroll deposit. Pat received interest on that loan and paid taxes on that interest, which was acceptable business practice. However, Pat had no idea that Carl had misappropriated the company's federal payroll taxes.

This two-count guilty plea required a preliminary meeting with the assigned federal judge. When the day arrived, Pat listened to the judge berate the prosecutor for originally indicting him on twenty-nine counts. The prosecutor offered a weak excuse, saying it was complicated.

Pat left the courtroom encouraged by the judge's remarks.

On the morning of that meeting, I received a text from Marthe, who related a dream she had during the night. She saw our family in vibrant colors: Pat wore purple, Andrew was clothed in orange, Alan wore blue, and I was adorned in green. Marthe wanted me to ask Pat if purple had any significance for him.

After Pat returned home, we headed to our lake property for a few hours of solace. As we drove, I remembered to tell him about Marthe's dream and her question. When I turned to speak to Pat, it struck me that he had changed clothes and now wore a deep purple shirt—one I had never seen! Surprised at his shirt choice, I asked if the color purple symbolized anything for him. He replied that he associated purple with Jesus' royalty. His answer satisfied me, but I wondered if there was more significance to my friend's dream.

When we arrived at the lake house, Pat searched the grounds and found the perfect-sized tree branch, which I wanted to place over our bed there. We hung the branch alongside two antique pictures of birds. Then we painted the words of Psalm 91:1 above the pictures. We had been clinging to this verse since the beginning of our ordeal: "He who dwells in the shelter of the Most High will rest in the shadow of the Almighty."

I further contemplated Marthe's dream, especially considering it had preceded Pat's meeting with the judge. I saw a disturbing comparison. Jesus was falsely accused and endured a mock trial before His crucifixion for sins He did not commit.

It was much later when I actually read that scene in the opening verses of John 19. The images and words now startled me: The Roman soldiers put a crown of thorns on Jesus' head and arrayed him in a purple robe! The chief priests and officers saw him and cried out, "Crucify! Crucify!" But Pilate answered, "As for me, I find no basis for a charge against him" (John 19:6).

# Chapter 4

# Empty Yet Full

*A time to mourn and a time to dance.*
ECCLESIASTES 3:4

As our first Christmas without Mom and Dad approached, I tried to get into the spirit of the holidays, but joy eluded me. It helped us to keep one tradition we had embraced as a family—purchasing and delivering gifts for a family in need.

The week before Christmas we took gifts to an elderly woman whose home we had helped repair through Blueprint Ministries. Yet we came away with something in return. Unprompted, and without knowing our circumstances, the woman spoke to us with authority. "Some people just get up and take a shower and start their day. Others are called to prayer," she said. "Have you had dark times? It's through the dark times that we see God more clearly, and our joy and strength are in Him alone."

Her words seemed inspired by God, and we left encouraged.

In the New Year, I sensed God prodding me to pray for my enemies. This challenge required loving them as He loves—and this is not easy! I prayed continually for God to remove my bitterness concerning Pat's former employer and others.

In the classic devotional book *My Utmost for His Highest,* Oswald Chambers wrote, "If God has made your cup sweet, drink it with grace; if he has made it bitter, drink it in communion with Him."[1] Accepting this cup and thanking God each day helped me cultivate a forgiving heart. But I still struggled.

Mary DeMuth says of forgiveness, "It's a holy letting-go, allowing God's justice to pervade the situation. And it releases you from bitterness and feeling like you have to punch."[2]

January meant an entire year had passed since the devastating day of Pat's indictment. It also marked a year since Pat and I had been visiting The Park Community Church, and we decided it was time to be more involved with the new church plant. This change meant leaving the comforts and familiarity of our longtime congregation and many dear friends. It also required a fresh commitment that included setting up chairs and a nursery for worship services in a rented space. Pat rose early on Sundays to drive his truck to a storage space to haul the church trailer filled with equipment. He was happy to serve in this way. I was happy to see him do what he does best.

Though I thanked God for carrying us through the turbulent past year, I sought spiritual refreshment by joining a book study offered by our church. In the book *Soul Feast,* these words soothed me: "Our confidence in the power of prayer is rooted in the promises that God is continually working for good in the midst of ambiguous situations and that God's purposes will prevail in the end."[3]

Several months passed without an indictment of Pat's employer, Carl. We prayed for the truth to be told so our lives could be restored. Meanwhile, we maintained Pat's business, grateful for the stability it provided, and we tried to go about life as normal.

For Pat, normal included getting another dog. He and Andrew trumped my objection to replacing Spencer so soon. They searched online and found "the cutest pup ever." Later in the day they brought home a six-week-old female mix—half Maltese, half poodle, and wholly adorable. Ellie Mae instantly brought a playful distraction to our home.

Summer arrived and included a family celebration of our niece's wedding, followed by a brief vacation. Since Andrew was an architecture student, Pat and I took him on a show-and-tell trip to Chicago. We delighted in his enthusiasm over details like the crossbeams of a building he had studied the previous semester.

But even on that fun trip, I couldn't manage to leave worry behind. On a boat tour of the city, I noticed a billboard with only one word—the federal prosecutor's last name. His name was displayed in white letters against a stark black background. The sight of this triggered fear in me. I later wrote in my journal: *God, please silence the attacks in my mind, and crush Satan before he crushes me.*

Back home from Chicago, Pat heard from his attorney that the prosecutor wanted to meet with me! This was an odd request, but Pat's attorney thought this personal interaction could benefit his case.

Pat took me to his attorney's office, where—with trepidation—I met the prosecutor, whose demeanor surprised me and put me at ease. He only needed Pat to cooperate, he said. His words assured me that he knew Pat was not involved in his employer's inner circle and that he was not out to punish Pat.

I hoped he was as truthful as he was reassuring.

In September, Pat and I went to Austin to join Alan and his girlfriend, Alix, for dinner to celebrate Alan's successful passing of his CPA exams. This occasion also helped us to sense that Alix might be "the one" for Alan, and this brought us both joy.

Arriving home that night, Pat needed to drop me off near the front door since he didn't have his garage door opener. While he drove around to the garage, I went through the house to unlock the back door. When I turned on the outside light for Pat, I noticed something through the door window. A five-foot-long snake reared its head toward me! I screamed to alert Pat, who ran for a hoe from the nearby shed. Then I watched through the window as he crushed the snake's head.

I couldn't help but think of my memory verse for that week's Bible study lesson. In Genesis 3:15, God spoke to the serpent: ". . . he will crush your head, and you will strike his heel."

The following week, after two years of waiting, we received the news that Pat's former employer had finally been arrested. We hoped this meant the evil parked at our doorstep would soon be crushed.

Though our future looked uncertain, Pat and I had the thrill of seeing Alan's future unfold. Alan had met Alix at A&M, where they both studied accounting. We noticed that Alix's calm, quiet demeanor provided a healthy balance to Alan's gregarious nature.

In early November, when Alan shared his intention to ask Alix to marry him, we weren't surprised. We listened to his plan to propose, and we happily agreed to host an engagement party after Christmas.

I love planning parties! I had hosted so many wedding showers for others in past years; now I could have a party for my own son and future daughter-in-law. This gave us something joyful to look forward to—and I so needed joy!

Another real blessing came around that same time. Andrew landed an internship with a Houston company for the spring semester. Since his degree plan required an internship, he was thrilled with the opportunity.

Both our boys were happy, which made me happy.

The following new year marked a long two years since the indictment. Pat and I, both weary in spirit, trudged through the winter months. We had at least one healthy distraction: we looked forward to an August wedding.

Alan and Alix asked our minister, Scott, to officiate the ceremony. When Scott arranged their marriage mentoring sessions with a couple from our church, Julie and Bobby, we discovered one more "God-incidence." Julie was the daughter of Larry, my Jesus-with-skin-on!

Pat and I were so thankful this couple would encourage Alan and Alix. I couldn't wait to tell Julie how God had used her father as a divine spokesman at a time I desperately needed to hear from God.

On the day I met Julie for lunch, her father had been hospitalized after a stroke. My account of the friendly and compassionate bookstore salesman, who unknowingly addressed all of my concerns, lifted Julie's spirit and made both of us cry.

Only one week later, Pat and I met Julie's family at Larry's funeral. During the standing-room-only service, I silently thanked God for the stranger who had touched my life.

June and July brought wedding showers and parties. Pat and I cherished our new friendship with Alix's parents, Dan and Connie. They did the bulk of the wedding planning, which would take place in their hometown of Austin.

I felt the natural emotional tugs expected of a mother-of-the-bride or groom, but I had so many emotions in addition to these! Just ten days before the wedding, I drove to Henderson because my parents' home had finally sold, eighteen months after going on the market. While Beth and I worked hard to clean and empty closets and cabinets, we laughed, cried, and enjoyed our special time together.

The following week, it was time to head to Austin for the big event. Pat and I left home on Thursday, two days before the wedding. While driving, he took a phone call from a coworker, who said the prosecutor had interviewed her earlier in the week. She wanted to let Pat know that she told the prosecutor of his complete innocence and that the prosecutor in turn assured her: Pat would be fine. They were not after Pat.

The timing of that call encouraged us as we hoped for a weekend of pure joy.

The wedding celebration felt surreal from the time we checked into the hotel—a grand, historic place. Our suite had an expansive balcony with wooden rocking chairs—the perfect spot for prayer and devotion. I prayed for God to "check in" before any of the guests arrived, to infuse this special occasion with His peace and presence.

On Friday evening, we joined the wedding party as we filed onto a chartered bus for the trip to the wedding rehearsal and dinner. My mind retreated to fond memories of loading many of these same young people—then children—onto school buses for field trips, and later (as teens) helping them on church buses for retreats and mission trips. This simple realization brought me joy.

At the wedding on Saturday, Alix looked like a princess-bride as she stood at the altar next to her enamored groom. After the ceremony, her father formally welcomed guests to the reception, and then Pat offered a prayer. My special honor was the mother-son dance. Alan and I had chosen the song "I Will Always Love You" by the Christian band Third Day. This song speaks of God's love for us before time began, and it perfectly expressed my love for Alan.

As we celebrated the evening away, I even danced with a tambourine that someone had handed me! After the reception, concerned that I might have appeared undignified, I asked Andrew his thoughts.

"Mom, we've been through a lot," he said. "You above anyone else should dance with the tambourine."

On my first morning back home, after sitting in my prayer chair and thanking God for the beautiful wedding, I couldn't believe the topic of the day's Bible reading—another perfectly timed verse. Jeremiah 31:3, 4 says: "I have loved you with an everlasting love; I have drawn you with loving-kindness. I will build you up. . . . Again you will take up your tambourines and go out to dance with the joyful."

I cried tears of joy. Dancing with a tambourine had been perfectly fine!

The wedding had been wonderful but exhausting. While the newlyweds headed off on their honeymoon, Pat and I took a few days to spend with Andrew. We left the stifling heat of South Texas to enjoy a friend's vacation home in a quaint town in Colorado.

The complete relaxation refreshed my spirit and energized me for a new project. Though I still helped Pat at his office part-time, I wanted to do something fresh and meaningful. As a former teacher, I always thought of August as the beginning of a new year.

When our pastor asked Dee Dee and me to teach a fall semester class on prayer, I jumped in, thrilled to work with my close friend on a subject so essential to me. We prayerfully collaborated as a team and carefully constructed a syllabus. In preparation, we read several books, including *The Ministry of Intercession* by Andrew Murray. Some of the author's words penetrated my soul:

> Blessed is the man who is not staggered by God's delay or silence or apparent refusal, but is strong in faith, giving glory to God. Such faith perseveres—importunately, if need be—and cannot fail to inherit the blessing.[4]

Dee Dee and I enjoyed teaching the evening class, which also gave us a weekly excuse to go out afterward for pancakes with Perry and Pat.

Pat became involved with our church as well. Besides his regular Sunday morning setup duty, he volunteered on behalf of the homeless. He also added meaningful work to his weekly schedule by assisting Perry, a commercial and residential contractor.

We welcomed those small but positive ventures as healthy distractions from our unresolved legal trouble. And our family life continued in a fairly normal way. While Andrew progressed through another year at A&M, Alan and Alix settled into a bungalow in one of Austin's older neighborhoods.

Yearning for the past made me depressed; anticipating the future made me anxious. In January, at the start of another new year, I asked God to renew my joy and help me live day by day, enjoying what each day brings.

So weary from wandering in this prolonged desert season, I focused on two Scriptures: ". . . take captive every thought to make it obedient to Christ" (2 Corinthians 10:5); and "The Lord himself goes before you and will be with you; he will never leave you nor forsake you. Do not be afraid; do not be discouraged" (Deuteronomy 31:8).

I desperately needed to shift my focus to the One who is mightier than the one throwing darts. Though I had become more aware of Satan's evil schemes, I remained fearful.

Now, three years after the helicopter invaded the space above our home, a fresh concern arrived. A co-conspirator with Carl refused to enter a guilty plea. This refusal meant a trial that would draw out the pain for our family. Our attorney said it would take a miracle for the man to plead guilty.

I woke up the next morning—the day the man's trial would begin—praising God and feeling His goodness. A few hours later Pat called with good news: the man had entered a guilty plea at six o'clock the night before.

We saw this turnaround as a miracle.

Our legal team continued to give us encouraging words: hold on; it's almost over; all is good; no need to worry; you can relax. Meanwhile, other men connected to Carl's various companies were implicated and indicted in the complex case.

Further encouragement came when Andrew received the offer of a second internship, in San Antonio, and the company would pay him a salary.

Support and affirmation from friends and God's Word continued as well. As we prayed for everyone involved in our case, we continued to claim the promise of Isaiah 26:3: "You will keep in perfect peace him whose mind is steadfast because he trusts in you."

And we continued.

Even in South Texas, January isn't the best time to plan a weekend at the lake with friends, but all of the couples in our Bible study were available at this time. As luck would have it, an ice storm hit our area the weekend we planned to go, but we still managed to come together for our visit. We enjoyed the rare opportunity to wear winter coats and gloves!

In the years before the indictment, the lake—like our family life—was full and flowing. But after three years of drought, instead of clear turquoise water lapping against the rocks, only a cracked and creviced landscape appeared. We longed for the refreshment the lake once offered us. Now it was a dry and desolate place, void of the sights and sounds of life at the lake. There was no swimming, fishing, boating, or cliff jumping.

Our group decided to cross the "lake" on foot. As we

walked on the dry lake bottom, I thought of how the Israelites must have felt crossing through the Red Sea. The symbolism overwhelmed me. My family had endured bondage for three years, and we hoped that God's deliverance was on its way.

# Chapter 5

# Powers of This World

*. . . in the place of justice—wickedness was there.*
ECCLESIASTES 3:16

After three difficult years of waiting for redemption, Pat and I began to feel an undercurrent of uncertainty in our attorney-client relationship. Just two weeks before the February sentencing date, at 9:30 in the evening, Pat's attorney called with an unexpected—indeed, last-minute—request. He wanted Pat to review a "letter of contrition" he had just e-mailed. He explained the prosecutor insisted on the letter, which was due on the judge's desk by 8:30 the next morning.

After reading the draft, Pat was angry. The content suggested undue contrition on his part. How could such a letter possibly benefit his case?

His attorney responded by saying the letter to the judge must include certain terminology, and the prosecutor would accept nothing less.

Pat could not understand this approach and challenged his attorney: "Why are we worried about what the prosecutor wants?"

The attorney assured him to trust their plan, that everything was fine. Pat cooperated by revising the letter in his own words.

Our misgivings amplified the following week when Pat learned about his legal team's plan to defend him. They reasoned that any defense would hurt the prosecutor's case against the guilty men.

"But I don't understand!" Pat could not hide his frustration from his attorney. "You've told me for three years to keep quiet, take it on the chin, and not defend myself to anyone, that all the false accusations would be explained once I could tell my story before the judge."

As Pat's day in court neared, he desperately wanted to tell the judge how his former employers hid their fraudulent activities from him, and completely so, knowing their scheme would not work if he had been aware of anything. However, Pat's legal team remained confident in their plan as the best course of action. They would fully cooperate with the prosecutor.

Pat and I needed more assurance than they could offer. We sought God with prayer for deliverance according to Psalm 50:15: "Call upon me in the day of trouble; I will deliver you, and you will honor me." We also prayed for those who falsely accused Pat, acknowledging the words of Jesus in Matthew 5:44: "Love your enemies and pray for those who persecute you." Concerning the media, we prayed the words of Isaiah 50:7: "Because the Sovereign Lord helps me, I will not be disgraced." And we asked for evil to be defeated according to Romans 16:20: "The God of peace will soon crush Satan under your feet."

On a Friday in late February, Pat and I entered the courtroom. He took a seat with his legal team, and I sat several rows back, along with four of Pat's closest friends and his brother Kenny. The room was packed. We stood at the call to "All rise," and the judge approached the bench.

After everyone was seated, we knew by the judge's irritated tone that something was terribly wrong.

In the judge's opening remarks—more like a soliloquy—he maintained that in a conspiracy everyone pays the penalty. In the assassination of Abraham Lincoln, the judge explained, John Wilkes Booth pulled the trigger, but many were hanged.

Within minutes, I sensed an oppressive evil in the room. I instinctively placed my hands over my head as if for protection.

Would the judge actually include Pat with the guilty men? Surely he couldn't believe Pat had been aware of any illegal activity. Two years earlier, when Pat reluctantly turned in his guilty plea, he heard this same judge berate the prosecutor for aggressively indicting Pat on so many counts. Had something changed the judge's mind?

Everything felt wrong. And everything ended wrong. The prosecutor did not honor his words to me.

The judge, following the prosecutor's lead, ignored our attorney's attempt to interject. He sentenced Pat to thirty-six months in a federal prison camp and ten million dollars in restitution. He further ordered Pat to report to the camp by June 9—of all days, our wedding anniversary.

This incredulous decision—with no evidence to support the verdict—violated Pat's written plea agreement.

The judge added insults to the injustice by scolding Pat, asserting he had surely fooled all of his friends (more than fifty people had written testimonial letters to the judge affirming Pat's integrity). The judge further displayed a bit of sarcasm by suggesting Pat could start a Bible study in prison. Then he interrupted his own rant to ask our attorney how a previously sentenced client was doing in prison.

Later, as I recalled the court proceedings, I saw a sickening irony. I remembered the start of Alan's sixth-grade year, when he looked forward to greater privileges in middle school. On the first day of class Alan was assigned to the Blue Birds, which was fine until he realized the Blue Birds weren't allowed any field trips. Yellow Birds, Red Birds, and Green Birds could go on field trips. But the previous year's Blue Birds had misbehaved on a trip, so the school took away the group's privileges for incoming Blue Birds. This decision, of course, made no sense.

My husband had been placed with the Blue Birds.

Pat's legal team had always expressed confidence that everything would be fine for him once Carl and any others were sentenced. Even the night before the sentencing, they assured Pat that his indictment would only serve to convict the others. But the guilty parties—perhaps strategically—had requested a delay of their sentencing, and they received a thirty-day extension.

Back home after the courtroom debacle, Pat was crushed to his core. We both suffered the shock of this blow and needed to trust in God's ability to help us. We could only pray the words of Mark 9:24, that God would help our unbelief.

Friends and family came to our home to mourn with us as if a death had occurred. They cried and prayed with us. Others sent words of support, expressing their faith that the Lord would sustain us as we held closely to Him.

For three days, I experienced mental confusion. I walked around the house bewildered, debilitated by grief, and unable to seek God in my usual morning prayer time. On the fourth day, out of habit and obedience, I dropped into my overstuffed armchair.

After asking God to sit close beside me, I admitted that I felt betrayed by Him. Psalm 46:10 quickly delivered His response: "Be still and know that I am God."

I continued to ask God why He allowed the prosecutor to betray us. Other faith questions began to flood my troubled mind: Why did God allow Satan to enter Judas to betray Jesus? Why did God's people—including Jesus, Joseph, Daniel, David, Paul, and Peter—suffer from false accusations?

My Jesus-with-skin-on, Larry, would have again directed me to the ninth chapter of John's Gospel. He would calmly remind me this calamity was all for the glory of God. Yet I might ask him in return: How can injustice glorify God?

Overwhelmed with sadness, I silently poured my heart out to God. I prayed Psalm 13:1-6:

How long, O Lord? Will you forget me forever? How long will you hide your face from me? How long must I wrestle with my thoughts and every day have sorrow in my heart? How long will my enemy triumph over me? Look on me and answer, O Lord my God. Give light to my eyes, or I will sleep in death; my enemy will say, "I have overcome him," and my foes will rejoice when I fall. But I trust in your unfailing love; my heart rejoices in your salvation. I will sing to the Lord, for he has been good to me.

Five days after the sentencing, our attorney filed a one hundred-page rebuttal that explained both the lack of evidence and the details omitted during the court proceedings. This legal document also requested a resentencing, which sparked a degree of hope for us.

But the prosecutor immediately shot back, threatening to make things even worse for Pat. The bully tactic worked. Pat's attorney withdrew the rebuttal that would have exposed the truth.

And our hopes were trampled.

Pat's attorney later surmised the prosecutor didn't want anything to interfere with the case against the guilty parties, who still awaited sentencing. He explained to us that a federal prosecutor does not have to abide by the same rules of engagement as we do.

Our eyes were opened to a system with tragic flaws.

Hoping a change of scenery would help, we drove to Austin the following weekend to spend time with Alan and Alix. On Sunday morning, we pulled ourselves together enough to attend a worship service at their church. Pat and I needed that hour of respite.

The pastor, who we'd never met, posed a question to the congregation: "What are you doing to advance the gospel and to seek justice?" He went on to say that justice implies action, which exposes evil. He ended his sermon with another question: "If we had a cure for cancer, would we go all out and share it with everyone?"

As I absorbed the pastor's words, I wondered if I would be willing to go all out to expose the evil I knew existed.

Pat's world had collapsed in an instant on that sentencing day. Words he never expected to hear filled him with distrust of all he knew to be true: that if you do the right thing, good things happen. But good things were not happening.

A full month had passed before Carl and his accomplice were sentenced. They each received 120 million dollars in restitution and twelve years in federal prison with an order to report immediately.

Our attorney offered us a fresh source of hope the following week by supplying the name of someone who specialized in fighting restitutions. Pat, full of despair, agreed to meet this attorney, Nancy.

Right away, Pat saw Nancy as someone willing to fight for him. She immediately saw something in Pat, too: fear and devastation. After denouncing the prosecutor's methods, she encouraged Pat to neither be afraid nor operate out of fear.

Over coffee the next morning, Pat told me about a strange dream he had: bulls chased him wherever he went. His nightmare made me recall the Scripture passage I read just an hour earlier. Chills ran through me as I retrieved my Bible to read Psalm 22:12-14, out loud, to Pat: "Many bulls surround me; strong bulls of Bashan encircle me. Roaring lions tearing their prey open their mouths wide against me. I am poured out like water, and all my bones are out of joint."

It seemed God's Word had supplied an interpretation of Pat's dream. The psalmist David portrays the threat of evildoers who encircle God's people. Verse 21 adds his prayer for deliverance: "Save me from the horns of the wild oxen."

We began to see Nancy as the one God might use to deliver us. She seemed determined to take the bulls by the horns.

Before I even met Nancy, and without realizing what I was saying, I asked Pat, "Where is the warrior's office?" I had subconsciously referred to Nancy as a warrior, like the angel-warrior in the Old Testament book of Daniel.

I reached for my Bible to find the story of the angel who intervened on Daniel's behalf:

> ". . . Do not be afraid, Daniel. Since the first day that you set your mind to gain understanding and to humble yourself before your God, your words were heard, and I have come in response to them. But the prince of the Persian kingdom resisted me twenty-one days" (Daniel 10:12, 13).

With amazement, I realized Pat first met Nancy twenty-one days after his sentencing.

Pat was eager for me to meet Nancy. Before we left home for her office, I photocopied a psalm to include in Pat's file. Wanting God's Word to physically sit among all the legal proceedings, I chose Psalm 35:1-9:

> Contend, O Lord, with those who contend with me; fight against those who fight against me. Take up shield and buckler; arise and come to my aid. Brandish spear and javelin against those who pursue me. Say to my soul, "I am your salvation." May those who seek my life be disgraced and put to shame; may those who plot my ruin be turned back in dismay. May they be like the chaff before the wind, with the angel of the Lord driving them away; may their path be dark and slippery, with the angel of the Lord pursuing them. Since they hid their net for me without cause and without cause dug a pit for me, may ruin overtake them by surprise—may the net they hid entangle them, may they fall into the pit, to their ruin. Then my soul will rejoice in the Lord and delight in his salvation.

Not knowing what to expect at this meeting with Nancy, Pat and I prayed in the car before entering her office. We asked God to encourage us through her. Having been struck down and perplexed at every turn, we desperately needed someone in our corner.

My heart pounded as I walked up the stairs. But when Nancy greeted us, my racing pulse settled a bit. Her no-nonsense appearance—including casual shoes—gave me the impression she'd be in this for the long haul. She would roll up her sleeves and work overtime if needed. I saw a look of dogged determination on her face.

Before Pat and I had shared our perception of the prosecutor with Nancy, she shared some strong views of her own. But then she reminded us to not make any decisions based on fear. We felt every decision we had made up to this point had been based on fear!

Nancy's next words caused Pat and me to look at each other. She said we needed to put on our full armor to fight this battle. Was God speaking to us through her?

When we got back in the car, we immediately said the same thing: "Ephesians 6!"

A verse from that chapter had become so real in the past months as we became aware of forces we had never encountered before this period. Ephesians 6:12 says, "For our struggle is not against flesh and blood, but against the rulers, against the authorities, against the powers of this dark world and against the spiritual forces of evil in the heavenly realms."

Before I got out of bed the next morning, barely awake in the darkness, my spirit sang the words of an old hymn: "Strength for today and bright hope for tomorrow; great is thy faithfulness, Lord unto me."[1] Later, in my devotion time, I opened to Psalm 63:6, 7. I could barely believe the words: "On my bed I remember you; I think of you through the watches of the night. Because you are my help, I sing in the shadow of your wings." These verses explained my spirit's singing, and this awareness sustained me that day—like manna from Heaven.

Some lines from the book *Mending Cracks in Your Soul* also spoke to me at this time: "When the Holy Spirit reveals the spiritual, He will give you the additional information that will comfort you and give you peace and security in the midst of the trauma."[2]

The Holy Spirit had my attention. We had an advocate!

On a warm day in March, Pat and I drove to a nearby park for a walk, but we grew thirsty since we hadn't thought to take water. On the return to our car, a young boy approached us from a distant water stand holding two cups of water. This unexpected kindness brought to life a verse Pat mentioned a few days earlier: "I provide water in the desert and streams in the wasteland, to give drink to my people, my chosen" (Isaiah 43:20). And, just before our walk, I had read about water in my devotion time. Psalm 74:15 says, "It was you who opened up springs and streams"; Psalm 78:15, 16 says, "He split the rocks in the desert and gave them water as abundant as the seas; he brought streams out of a rocky crag and made water flow down like rivers."

Other scriptural references to water had been coming to me for days. One friend randomly sent two verses in one e-mail. First, she shared Isaiah 41:17, 18: "The poor and needy search for water, but there is none; their tongues are parched with thirst. But I the Lord will answer them; I, the God of Israel, will not forsake them. . . . I will turn the desert into pools of water, and the parched ground into springs." Then she added

Isaiah 48:21: "They did not thirst when he led them through the deserts; he made water flow for them from the rock; he split the rock and water gushed out."

Those verses served to remind God's people of His provision during their years in the desert as recorded in the Old Testament. "Then Moses raised his arm and struck the rock twice with his staff. Water gushed out, and the community and their livestock drank" (Numbers 20:11).

When Pat and I returned home from the park that day, we saw water gushing out of the ground like a fountain—a broken sprinkler head! In the midst of this craziness I received a text message from yet another friend, who felt led to share a verse with us. Psalm 105:41 says, "He opened the rock, and water gushed out; like a river it flowed in the desert."

It seemed obvious to us that God provided this repetition, in word and in deed, to make His promises quite clear. He could—and would—sustain us.

Soon enough, the timing of this encouragement would prove significant. God knew what the prosecutor planned to throw at us in the weeks ahead.

# Chapter 6

# Dealing with Daggers

*Though he slay me, yet will I hope in Him. . . .*
*Indeed, this will turn out for my deliverance.*

JOB 13:15, 16

April brought further encouragement by phone, e-mail, texts from friends, and through God's Word—so real to us in this fresh trouble. We heard anguish in the voices and words of those who shared our pain. As we all absorbed the reality of our circumstances, we lacked protocol for how to comfort each other.

Though I felt like isolating myself, even from friends, Pat and I decided to join his Bible study men and their wives for a weekend retreat. While there, I read a psalm of lament I could have written myself. Psalm 102:6, 7 says, "I am like a desert owl, like an owl among the ruins. I lie awake; I have become like a bird alone on a roof." At that point, I stopped to read the commentary on the two verses: "Don't reject help and conversation. Suffering silently is neither Christian nor particularly healthy. Instead, graciously accept the support and help from family and friends."[1]

That Sunday, we headed to Austin and attended church with Alan and Alix. Pen in hand, I anticipated hearing from God that morning. The pastor's message, from Genesis 22, the story of Abraham and Isaac, stressed that our most important tests are the most illogical ones. The One who tests us is also the One who provides, the pastor explained. He ended his sermon with the reminder that God often does His best work during the hardest tests of our lives.

Another weekend, Pat drove to our lake house to seek refuge through his normal outdoor chores. As he walked the property, Pat saw a large snake slithering through the grass alongside the garage. He ran into the garage for a hoe and soon chopped off the serpent's head.

Later, checking on the water well, Pat bent down to open the small door of the pump house when a bobcat jumped from the balcony above the garage and landed only three feet from Pat's face. The wild animal ran off without attacking him, but the threat unnerved Pat since we hadn't seen a bobcat in the twelve years we owned the property!

A few days later I came upon the words of Psalm 91:13-15: "You will tread upon the lion and the cobra; you will trample the great lion and the serpent. 'Because he loves me,' says the Lord, 'I will rescue him; I will protect him, for he acknowledges my name. He will call upon me, and I will answer him; I will be with him in trouble, I will deliver him and honor him.'"

Even with these signs of God's protection, I continued to worry. In my journal, I wrote:

*I see your promises of rescue and restoration in the Bible, and I want to claim them, but my mind won't let me. I have been clinging to your Word and your signs for three years, and I feel so defeated. You revealed Bar-Jesus to me. Is evil crushing us? Please lift this burden. Remove our confusion and devastation. Increase my awareness of your presence with me. Remind me to sing praises to you.*

Though Pat escaped the snake and the bobcat, he suffered a serious financial injury only days later. Due to his unmerited sentencing, Pat's commission-based earnings—his entire income—ended without notice.

We prayed specifically for God to go before us according to Genesis 50:20—that God would use for good the evil intended to harm us. Shortly after our prayer, a friend sent me a text with a verse she believed God supplied in her prayer time: Genesis 50:20. Again!

That morning, I sang in my spirit the words from an old hymn, " . . . my anchor holds within the veil." I searched through my hymnal until I found the song title: "My Hope Is Built." As I read the second verse, I felt the Holy Spirit had surely led me there:

When darkness veils his lovely face, I rest on his unchanging grace. In every high and stormy gale, my anchor holds within the veil. On Christ the solid rock I stand, all other ground is sinking sand.[2]

I needed to hold tightly to my anchor in the storm to keep from being battered by waves of doubt.

Later that day I met my friend Bonnie for lunch. She wanted to tell me about the image of our family she had seen in her prayer earlier: encased in glass, we were surrounded by angels. She explained it as strikingly picturesque, complete with twinkling lights. After we prayed before eating our lunch, Bonnie looked at me and said, "Luann, as we prayed just now, I saw a large anchor with you and Pat."

Coincidental? I prefer providential. The anchor in the old hymn references Hebrews 6:19 and 20: "We have this hope as an anchor for the soul, firm and secure. It enters the inner sanctuary behind the curtain, where Jesus, who went before us, has entered on our behalf." Bonnie's prayer visions repeated the promises of God's intervention and protection for us.

When Pat called Nancy about the loss of our income, he found she had already addressed the problem. She believed this latest development could work to our benefit by serving to reveal the integrity of Pat's personal business.

The next day we met with Nancy to understand exactly what we faced. While there, Andrew called to let us know he couldn't use his ATM card. Nancy knew exactly what was happening: the government had seized our funds. Between this and our sudden loss of income, what would we do? We felt that evil forces were ramping up against us. Our warrior-attorney began making phone calls.

With sinking hearts, Pat and I drove several blocks to Dee Dee's office at the nearby headquarters of Blueprint Ministries, where we had served as volunteers. She met us in the chapel and prayed over us as we knelt at the altar. I wanted to stay right there with my head on the communion rail. I needed Jesus to take away our pain and suffering.

The next morning, a friend sent me a verse about Gideon's

altar: "But the Lord said to him, 'Peace! Do not be afraid. You are not going to die.' So Gideon built an altar to the Lord there and called it The Lord is Peace" (Judges 6:23, 24).

I realized our similarity to Gideon in this battle. His clan was the weakest and the least—exactly the way we felt against the federal government. God used Judges 6:12, 13 to speak further to me: "When the angel of the Lord appeared to Gideon, he said, 'The Lord is with you, mighty warrior.' 'But sir,' Gideon replied, 'if the Lord is with us, why has all this happened to us?'"

Gideon couldn't quite believe God's promise of favor; he needed more assurance. We did too.

The prosecution team came at us with a vengeance after our appeal motion was filed. First, they asserted that we spent money frivolously. Their two examples to the judge included our monthly deposit to Andrew's college account for his living expenses and our monthly amount of giving to our church. These expenditures—the exact same amounts for the past three years—were neither unusual nor extravagant.

Next, the prosecutor delayed the court hearing on the release of our funds. He then gave notice to Nancy: if she moved forward with the appeal, Pat would be held in contempt of court, which would deny his right to an appeal. These tactics were meant to inflict fear and panic. And they did.

The prosecutor also tried to intimidate Nancy by threatening to seize her office bank accounts to recover the legal fees we had paid her. This threat forced Nancy to seek guidance from yet another attorney.

Meanwhile, the clock kept ticking. Pat's surrender date

loomed in less than thirty days, June 9, our thirtieth wedding anniversary. We were anxious to see if the judge would allow an appeal and, if granted, an extension, so Pat could remain at home during the process.

It frustrated us to learn the judge actually consulted the prosecutor—who we now viewed as Bar-Jesus—regarding our request for the extension. The man who had assured us that Pat was only helping the government's case against the guilty men now appeared to show his true colors: he recommended that Pat report to prison on the original date.

I boldly asked God to intervene on our behalf and prayed the words of Habakkuk 3:2: "Lord, I have heard of your fame; I stand in awe of your deeds, O Lord. Renew them in our day, in our time make them known; in wrath remember mercy." I begged God to honor our Daniel defiance. I asked Him to give us an Ezra reversal, a Gideon victory, a David triumph, a Joshua win, a Joseph vindication, and a Job restoration.

I recalled some words about depending on God from a reflection on John 15:4 in the devotional book *Jesus Today*: "It's essential to remember that this inner strength comes through Me, through your connection with Me. . . . This promise is a powerful antidote to fear—especially your fear of being over-whelmed by circumstances you see looming ahead."[3]

Pat and I prayed for God to help us trust in His sovereignty. And then we watched to see what He would do.

We soon heard that the judge did not give in to the prosecutor. He granted Pat a thirty-day extension, moving the report date to July 9.

Much more importantly, he ruled in favor of Pat's right to an appeal.

We thanked God for His intervention. With our legal efforts moving forward, Pat and I had something to hope for.

And the extension made us breathe easier for a while.

Around this time, we received hopeful words from an eighty-two-year-old prayer warrior. A friend called and apologized for waiting three months to relay the message from her mother-in-law, Marion, who had interceded for us on that February day in court. After the outcome of that awful day, Marion believed the Lord gave her words on our behalf: "If you can stand the pull, there is nothing God can't pull you through. And your afflictions are working for you."

My friend had waited to share the message because of our distraught condition in those first weeks after Pat's sentencing. Now we seized on Marion's words and repeated them mentally each day. We desperately needed to believe we would get through this legal nightmare and that God would somehow bring good things out of it.

In the past twelve weeks, we'd certainly been pulled in every direction. And we faced new afflictions each day. That encouraging message would stay in our spirits in the days ahead as the words gained significance.

We experienced God's manifest presence through the outpouring of love from friends and family. Other encouragements sometimes came to us unexpectedly, as in the case of Maribel, who worked at the dry cleaners near our neighborhood.

In our regular visits to the cleaners, Pat and I couldn't help but notice Maribel's beauty—inside and out. Originally from Mexico City, her strong accent served to enhance her energetic personality. We could easily imagine her as a heavenly character from the former TV series *Touched by an Angel*.

Stopping by the cleaners shortly after the arrest of Pat's former employer, I received a card Maribel had waiting for me with a gift certificate enclosed! This surprised me since our friendship—until that time—consisted only of small talk, like the weather.

"Luann," she said, "in my prayer time I felt the Lord speaking to me to bless you and your husband. It was very strong, and I am just being obedient."

Back home, I read Maribel's words:

*I hope you can take strength in knowing you are a constant and beautiful light in this world. Enjoy having each other and open your hearts to all that God has planned for you. He never makes mistakes, even though sometimes we do not understand. Our heavenly Father does all things well.*

I later asked Maribel if she knew about our situation.

"I was not aware of your circumstances, but you need to know that God loves you and Pat so much, and it is a privilege to have Him use me to speak to you," she said.

Spiritual blessings such as this made us believe that God would indeed pull us through.

On Memorial Day weekend, we wanted to celebrate Andrew's twenty-third birthday in a normal way. We chose a family favorite, a day trip to Sea World, just twenty miles from our house. We braved the holiday crowd at the theme park on a hot, humid Saturday. However, just inside the park gate, my tears began to fall as I recalled our family times here when the boys were young. I tried without success to hide my sorrow behind sunglasses. We were supposed to be having fun, but I couldn't stop crying.

We sought relief and refuge from the heat in a shaded

area of a small stadium, where we awaited the Beluga whale show. Before the program began, Pat and I simultaneously noticed something remarkable: a single male cardinal. The bird remained completely still as it perched on a high wire used for acrobatic performances. As if instructed, he remained there while we fixed our eyes on him in wonder. When he flew away, his bright red wings flapped just over our heads.

I thanked God for reminding us of His presence in the midst of our pain. His gift of the cardinals had provided me with so much comfort in recent years. Now I was able to enjoy the remainder of our day at the park.

Only days later, I would need another dose of comfort. I reclined on my bed one afternoon, following the advice of a concerned friend who suggested daily rest. She used the analogy of open-heart surgery to say I was still on the operating table. I tried to rest for at least an hour each day and used the downtime to read inspiring Christian fiction. I gained encouragement from stories that showed God's intervention—books with happy endings. However, as I read on this day, a realization hit me: *Of course God can make Himself known in this story. It's fiction!* This sudden lapse of faith made me feel abandoned by God. Fresh tears made it impossible to continue reading.

Hearing a tapping sound, I turned my head toward the bedroom door that led to the patio. On the outside doorknob perched a beautiful redbird. I sat upright to get a better look. The male cardinal stretched his neck so that his face appeared perfectly framed in the door's square windowpane. The beautiful bird lingered a few moments—as if to make sure I saw him—before he flew away.

Birds often perch near windows, but I had never seen one on a doorknob! And the arrival of this cardinal, when I felt so lost and forgotten by God, seemed an undeniable sign of His goodness.

On the ninth of June, Pat and I celebrated our thirtieth anniversary despite the uncertainties. With his appeal in the works, we had some hope of deliverance. Even though I became sick, we felt grateful to be together on a day when Pat originally would have had to report to prison. With amazing timing, a friend from out of town arranged for a meal to be delivered to us from one of our favorite restaurants. Jana had no idea it was our anniversary or that I was sick. God, of course, did know.

In a mid-June journal entry, I recorded my anxious thoughts to God.

> I have little strength because I have little peace. I have little peace because I have little joy. Renew my mind. Revive my spirit. Restore my soul.

I felt stuck in a holding pattern, like a passenger on a plane, circling in turbulence, waiting to make a safe landing. Trapped in our circumstances, I cried, prayed, and hunkered down in search of God's presence. I savored my prayer-chair time alone with Him each morning—often the only peaceful hours of the day. While I had to relive our painful story to others, I could meet with God as a familiar friend who needed no background information or updates about our case.

I also savored my time at the piano. Before our world shattered, I had looked for a classical piano teacher who could help me relearn the collegiate level pieces I once played. Now, when I really needed it, God seemed to supply the perfect teacher, a woman with a doctorate in piano. My lessons began in late April, two months after Pat's sentencing.

Piano practice offered a positive diversion and also rekindled my passion for music. It took every ounce of my concentration to work on intricate passages in the Mozart and Beethoven sonatas. The structure of these classical pieces served to satisfy my longing for order and beauty. Also, it buoyed my spirit to hear the teacher say, "Luann, that was excellent."

Interestingly, I found myself playing Bach inventions that required the right hand to play staccato—fast—while the left hand played legato—slow—and not necessarily in sync. This pattern was much like my current reality. In life, as in music, I prefer Mozart, where the right and left hands complement each other.

The holding pattern continued, but I believed God could bring us through to a safe landing. I echoed the psalmist David's words: "Why are you downcast, O my soul? Why so disturbed within me? Put your hope in God, for I will yet praise him" (Psalm 42:5).

We encountered this same theme at church the following Sunday when our pastor gave a sermon on John 11. He specifically focused on the four days Mary and Martha waited for Jesus to show up after the death of their brother, Lazarus. We too were waiting for Him "to show up." I took note of Jesus' words concerning Lazarus: "This sickness will not end in death. No, it is for God's glory so that God's Son may be glorified through it" (John 11:4). Like Mary and Martha, Pat and I needed God's revelation in the midst of our devastation.

In Eric Metaxas' book *Miracles*, he discusses the resurrection of Lazarus.

> For God to be glorified, it sometimes means first allowing something unpleasant to transpire. Jesus could have saved Lazarus from dying, or could have raised him from the dead immediately, but he did not. In a sense this miracle shows us that we can trust God, and if we do trust him he might take us on the long and difficult road, but it's only to bless us the more in the long run. Can it be that God allows us to go through things specifically so that we have an opportunity to trust him and then to see him do something we wouldn't have expected, something beautiful and extraordinary that wouldn't have been possible if we had had our prayers answered?[4]

Pat and I desired to give God glory, but our suffering hindered our efforts. Though we continued to look to God for help, we grew weary of the struggle against injustice. "I am worn out calling for help; my throat is parched. . . . I am forced to restore what I did not steal" (Psalm 69:3, 4). Such words of lament from the psalms comforted us and brought an awareness of our omnipresent God.

One morning during the time we awaited the judge's decision about releasing our funds, my friend Vicki stopped by to pray with me. As we sat on the screened-in patio, a soft rain began to fall. While we prayed, the trickle became a steady stream, and then the stream became a flood.

Since our area was experiencing a severe drought, this trickle-stream-flood encouraged me. When the rain stopped,

I said to Vicki: "Wouldn't it be wonderful to have a cardinal appear?" Within minutes, a bright redbird perched in a tree where I'd never seen one before. The cardinal, coupled with the rain, once again refreshed my spirit.

## Chapter 7

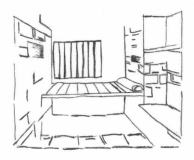

# Surprise Suffering

*Dear friends, do not be surprised at the painful trial you are suffering, as though something strange were happening to you. But rejoice that you participate in the sufferings of Christ, so that you may be overjoyed when his glory is revealed.*

1 PETER 4:12, 13

Pat and I remained in limbo as we waited on the judge regarding our attorney's requests to both release our funds and allow Pat to stay at home during the appeal.

I sought solace from a favorite book, *Blessing Your Spirit*:

There will be seasons when the enemy will prevail and it seems that God is not intervening, but I beg you to look with your spirit at the Ancient of Days who transcends those short seasons when He allows the enemy to act as though he is in control. You are in the eye of the Ancient of Days. He watches you. He cares for you. He is not grooming you for survival, but for triumph.[1]

For now, however, the enemy seemed to be prevailing. As June turned to July, the days were especially difficult for Pat. His glass-half-full outlook had shattered, releasing a flood of tears that could not be stopped.

As the head of our home, Pat had always put Alan, Andrew, and me before his own needs. Now, besides agonizing over the pain ahead for us and the rest of our family, he dreaded the prospect of going to an awful place.

As we waited for the judge to make the two crucial decisions, I recorded a prayer in my journal: *Father, I'm sad and I'm scared. Minister to my soul. You know what we need.*

But at this point, as at other times, I felt inadequate in my prayers—too weak to pray with confidence. When I shared my anguish in a text to a friend, asking her to pray, she replied with verses from Daniel 10:16-18.

> I said to the one standing before me, "I am overcome with anguish because of the vision, my lord, and I am helpless. How can I, your servant, talk with you, my lord? My strength is gone and I can hardly breathe." Again the one who looked like a man touched me and gave me strength. "Do not be afraid, O man highly esteemed," he said. "Peace! Be strong now; be strong."

In this passage, Daniel addressed the angel who rescued him after a twenty-one-day delay caused by spiritual forces. My friend's message spoke directly to my inability to pray well, and it further encouraged me since she knew nothing about the connection of these verses to Pat's first meeting with Nancy, twenty-one days after his sentencing.

As we waited to be rescued, we prayed against unforeseen obstacles that might hinder any angel working on our behalf. And we tried to carry on with the tasks at hand.

Meanwhile, our attorney told us we could hear something

from the judge at any time concerning our requested extension. Without it, Pat had less than a week before he would have to report to a federal correctional institution two hours south of San Antonio.

Although difficult to face, we needed a plan in case Pat had to leave us.

Pat asked his brother Kenny and a close friend, Mitch, to drive him to the prison camp—if necessary. We also realized that Pat should go to Pasadena, near Houston, without delay in order to spend time with his mom and his brother Rod. We made the trip together on the weekend before the report date.

Back home that Sunday—three days before Pat was scheduled to leave—we worshiped at our church. Afterward we visited a couple who had recently lost their twenty-two-year-old son, a young man who'd grown up with Andrew and frequented our home for weekly Bible study. We mourned our friends' loss without speaking of our clock-ticking situation. Their grief took precedence over our pain.

In the afternoon, we drove to Austin to be with Alan and Alix, who had just returned from a ten-day vacation with her family. Alan needed the personal time to say goodbye to his dad in case the extension was denied.

On Monday, with an uncomfortable quiet that meant no word of reprieve from the judge, we prepared for Pat's imminent departure. We asked God to fill us with His peace and go before us in all things.

Pat and I did not sleep at all during the hot July night before he left home. In the darkness, we prayed, cried, and held each other close. How could we accept that our God would not rescue us from such wrong?

Andrew did not sleep either. Instead, he poured his heart out in a letter. Early that morning, he brought it to his dad and watched as he read it.

> *Never did I think I would be writing this letter to you, but we have been given a trial that is purely of evil and of this world. I am not that good at going to the Bible when in need, but I did this time. Nothing can make this better, but knowing that God takes care of the ones who praise him is reassuring. Even though the last thing I want to do is praise God.*
>
> *Paul and Silas were unjustly thrown in jail, and they sang hymns of praise to God and all the doors were opened and the chains were broken. Peter, also unjustly thrown in jail, had the church praying fervently for him (as you do), and God sent an angel to open the door and bring him out. Noah faced being asked to build an ark while God wiped the earth clean, and he never took his eyes off God.*
>
> *Shadrach, Meshach, and Abednego chose to not bow down to the king, yet when the king looked back he saw three men walking around in the fire unharmed, with a fourth guy looking like a heavenly being. And you have been unjustly thrown into the fire, yet I know God will send an angel to take care of you.*
>
> *Job (my go-to Bible character for my life) faced trials where God takes away his children, property, wealth, his good name, and his health. After that, God allows Satan to afflict Job, but God is not punishing Job. It says God called him "blameless and upright" (you), but Job suffers because he is among the best of men. God knew he could take it. Job's response? He falls to the ground on his knees in worship.*
>
> *Dad, when this is all over, I know God will gladly say to you, "Well done, good and faithful servant!" (Matthew 25:21)*

After reading, Pat hugged Andrew and they cried together. Then, honoring Pat's wishes, Andrew left for work as usual.

A few minutes later, Pat received an e-mail letter from Alan, who was hurting, and wishing he could be with us. Alan, like Andrew, comforted Pat with his words:

*I want to let you know how honored and blessed I feel to be your son. I am so proud of you for not only fighting this sentence but for leading our family through something that no one else has experienced. My whole life you have been telling me how proud you are of me, but I have bragged to my friends about how lucky I am to have a dad like you.*

*There's never been a doubt that you have kept your hope not in your lawyers or the process but in the Lord, which would explain your unexplainable optimism at times, because you know that the Lord has not given up and forsaken us. Instead He has prepared a way that we just can't see yet. You have given an incredible example of how to love your family and friends in the face of adversity. You have also given an incredible example of how to be a supporting and leading husband, something I am trying to follow.*

*I know these next few days will be challenging, but I wanted to assure you that we will be alright. Andrew and I have grown so close through this whole process and not only will we be taking care of Mom, but so will Mom's 100 friends.*

*God has blessed us immensely, and I know it is hard to see it through the anger and frustration, but I am praying that blessings will be revealed once this new chapter starts.*

After reading, Pat called Alan, and they too cried together. This surreal morning also included Pat's mother, who came from Houston despite our recent visit; she wanted to be with us at this time. Kenny and Wendye drove down from Austin, and by mid-morning, Andrew had rejoined us—too distraught to stay at work.

When Mitch arrived, the time had come.

Pat found me in the back of the house, where I had retreated, unwilling to see him drive away. We said our good-byes in private. As I hugged him—not wanting to let go—I uttered the words of a familiar hymn, "Onward Christian Soldier." We both knew he would not be alone in this battle; God would go with him.

For the next two days, I had neither the strength nor the desire to meet with God in my morning prayer time. By the third day, I returned to my routine: coffee, Bible, journal in hand.

Though I remained angry and disappointed, reluctant to talk to God, I picked up my journal and wrote out my prayer: *I need fresh manna today.* I soon realized that God was not reluctant to talk to me. He spoke through Jeremiah 31:25: "I will refresh the weary and satisfy the faint." I further felt His encouragement as I read from *The Complete Works of E. M. Bounds on Prayer*, especially these lines: "The praying Christian is like a brave soldier who, as the conflict grows more severe, exhibits more courage. When delay and denial come, he increases his earnest asking and does not stop until prayer prevails."[2]

I prevailed through that day and the next.

But then I crashed.

On Sunday I woke up with no physical reserves. My emotional pain was affecting my whole body. My spirit cried out: *Are you there, God? Am I crazy to believe that you hear me, and that you are all that you say you are?*

Going outside for some fresh air before the day grew too hot, I saw a mess of leaves around the pool. I grabbed a broom to sweep up the debris and release some of my anxiety. As if waiting for me, a single male cardinal appeared at the pool's edge—just where I could see him. His arrival was a tender reminder that God was with me.

When an entire week passed without hearing from Pat, we began to worry. Nancy told us the delay was not unusual, that Pat needed his commissary services set up in order to receive phone and e-mail privileges.

Kenny assured us Pat was in a good place. He showed us a brochure of available activities at the correctional camp. We relieved our worries by humor, saying Pat would teach others the most efficient way to do the task at hand. However, each passing day grew more difficult as we waited to hear from Pat. Nothing felt right.

On the seventh day I ventured out, trying to carry on as if things were normal—at a time when nothing was normal. At the grocery store, a clerk unknowingly encouraged me when she mentioned how the cooling breeze outside lets us know God is with us. Next, I got a haircut, which always makes me feel better. Afterward, when I stopped at the cleaners, Maribel announced that my dry cleaning was paid for—a gift. She told me not to worry; God is our provider.

In the late afternoon, our friend and financial advisor stopped by to alert me that our assets, including our retirement accounts, had been frozen. With Maribel's words in mind, I remained calm, which surprised him.

The phone call we had waited a week for finally came that evening as Andrew and I drove across town to meet friends for dinner. When my cell phone rang, we suddenly heard Pat's voice through the car speaker. I began to cry and had to pull off the road into the nearest parking lot.

"We only have fifteen minutes to talk," Pat said with urgency, yet without panic. "I don't want you to be worried or upset." After Pat's continual distress in his last weeks at home, he now sounded so calm and strong that I almost didn't recognize his voice.

"God is in control," he said. "But I'm in solitary confinement." My heart raced as I took in those last words, and I struggled to breathe. Andrew took my hand, and we tried to focus on Pat's every word. After reassuring us he was safe and God was with him, Pat asked me to write down a message for Nancy. I grabbed a pen and the brown paper sleeve of a Starbucks coffee cup—the only thing I could find to write on.

Pat explained that after he checked into the camp he learned that both Carl and his accomplice were inmates at the same facility! This unforeseen circumstance would complicate Pat's pending appeal since any communication with these men could be a problem. The only solution was to request a transfer to another facility.

The camp administrator addressed the issue by calling the prosecutor, who said Pat would have to go to "special housing." Pat complied, not knowing this meant solitary confinement—a lockdown facility for disciplinary action.

Within his first two hours at the camp, Pat found himself in a twelve-by-eight-foot cell where he could not leave without being handcuffed. A one-square-foot window provided his only view: a corridor with a wall phone. Pat had begged an entire week for permission to use this phone to call either his attorney or me.

As the fifteen minutes came to a close, Pat prayed for our family and then began to say goodbye. When his voice cut off in mid-sentence, my pent-up emotions turned to hysteria.

Andrew got out of the car to take my place at the wheel and then called our friends to cancel our dinner plan. We turned around to head home.

In my distress, I called my friend Patti for prayer. She answered right away and remained calm while trying to understand my words between heaving sobs and gasping for air. Though Andrew took the phone to explain Pat's situation, Patti's concern and prayer focused on me. She feared I was having an emotional breakdown.

Back home, I collapsed in a den chair and began to calm down. Andrew brought me water and something to eat. He also contacted family members and Nancy.

As if he was the parent and I the child, Andrew tried to assure me everything was fine. He tucked me into bed early that night, prayed, and rested beside me until I fell asleep.

The next day I received a letter that Pat had told us to expect. He had written in pencil, having no access to a pen. With no commissary privileges yet, he used an uncancelled stamp from another letter. He shared some good news: he was able to get a Bible on his second day of confinement. He also explained that receiving regular phone access depended on his assigned counselor—who was away on vacation.

The rest of Pat's letter pierced me:

*In my time of total despair, I wondered why God wouldn't even let me get a message to you, so you could have some sense of peace and be able to pass it along to the boys.*

*But then a huge, peaceful sensation came over me. I don't know if it was the words from the book of Job I was reading or not being able to use the phone just outside my door. Maybe it was the way I fell into this mess without knowing what happened or not being able to turn off my own light, but the sensation soothed my mind and let me know I'm not in control, God is.*

*That is what I most desperately want you to know. God's got this! He is speaking to me every day. He's not only telling me, but He is showing me that we are going to get through this.*

While Pat's words about God's presence comforted me, my heart ached for him. I prayed before attempting to write back. Realizing that God's Word would connect us, I began my letter by suggesting we read the same chapters of the Bible each day. We could begin with 1 Peter, where I had just read a verse that comforted me concerning Pat: "For it is commendable if a man bears up under the pain of unjust suffering because he is conscious of God" (1 Peter 2:19).

Until a new letter arrived, I read Pat's first one over and over. As the days passed, I recalled Marion's words: "If you can stand the pull, there is nothing God can't pull you through; your afflictions are working for you." It seemed as if Pat and I were being tested beyond reason. We prayed that our harsh afflictions were somehow working for us.

In another letter, Pat shared an unusual incident. A guard he'd never seen before came to his cell and told him to hang in there; everything was going to be fine. The guard seemed different than the others, Pat wrote, with kind eyes that looked into your soul. Pat sensed he was a messenger from God, and this brought him further peace.

Pat also shared a heartwarming story about a man in the solitary cell beside him, Casper, who wanted to be friends with Pat. Though they could not see one another, they spoke outside during their one hour of weekday recreation time in a fenced area. Casper asked if Pat would be his "cellie"—a term Pat had never heard. If solitary confinement became crowded, Casper wanted Pat to be with him!

I believed Casper had quickly picked up on what others already knew about Pat: that you want him to be your friend. But I wanted Pat to be *my* cellie!

And so, the reality of things hit me: Pat was spending each day alone in a concrete and metal box with one small interior window void of sunlight while I remained in our comfortable home. Yet he had a measure of peace, and I was frantic. He felt secure; I felt paralyzed, unable to concentrate on anything other than getting him out of that lockdown situation.

Nancy was out of town when Pat first called, but she responded by making phone calls to push for his transfer. She requested another federal camp, in Bastrop, Texas, about 100 miles northeast of San Antonio. Meanwhile, Pat's guards told him it could take a month to process the necessary paperwork for his transfer. A month!

Considering Pat's extreme circumstances, the thought of going to church that next Sunday didn't seem right. But not going didn't feel right either. Andrew and I decided to offer our hearts to God in the backyard, attending church-by-the-pool—with smoothies. He selected a sermon podcast by a favorite pastor, and we gathered our Bibles, journals, and his phone with podcast speakers.

The message we heard closed with the meaningful lyrics of a Chris Tomlin song, "Whom Shall I Fear (God of Angel Armies)."

# Chapter 8

# Protection and Provision

*The Lord replied, "My presence will
go with you, and I will give you rest."*
EXODUS 33:14

"You have a collect call from an inmate at a correctional facility. Will you accept this call?"

I eagerly answered yes to the recorded message.

"Luann! I'm in San Antonio."

"Pat, is it really you? Are you out of lockdown?"

"I just arrived at the Bexar County facility, and I'm alone in a waiting room while they process my paperwork. Oh . . . I am so happy to finally talk to you."

After I'd waited five days to hear my husband's voice again, tears ran down my face. I feared his transfer could take a month, so this surprise overwhelmed me with relief. Strangely, it seemed like good news to know he was in the local jail! Even though I couldn't visit him there, we could now talk without restrictions, which we did, four or five times this same day.

In the late afternoon—capping the day—I received a visit from yet another male cardinal. His swooping past the den window reminded me of God's presence. Besides this comfort, I could anticipate talking to Pat again in the morning.

The next call included hearing about Pat's noteworthy introduction to the county detention center. The admissions staff had taken more than ten hours to process his paperwork. It was 10:30 p.m. before a guard escorted Pat to his assigned floor.

However, during Pat's long hours in the waiting room, a man stopped by to ask the clerk if anyone had signed up for his scheduled Bible study that evening. When the clerk answered no, Pat spoke up to say he would love to participate in a study, though he had no Bible since he had to leave everything behind in the solitary cell at the prison camp.

The man sat down with Pat and they began a discussion of Nicodemus, a secret follower of Jesus (John 3). The lesson focused on giving God control of your life. Before leaving, the man told Pat he would get him a Bible by the next day.

Pat didn't have to wait that long. When he finally reached his floor that night, he opened a trunk at the foot of his bunk bed and found a Bible. When he asked the inmates if everyone received a Bible, they shook their heads and said the man before him must have left it.

That long first day at the jail wasn't over yet. After thirteen days of isolation, Pat eagerly accepted some inmates' offer of a late-night card game. And the men were kind to him.

On Pat's third day, as I hauled the trash receptacles to the curb for pickup, I turned back to the house just in time to see a familiar visitor. A cardinal flew at a steady pace toward me from the far end of the driveway. He swooped just inches from my face and seemed to pause, midair, before perching in a nearby bush. The beautiful sight produced tears of gratitude. I saw how God was tending to both my needs and Pat's in unique ways.

But those bits of encouragement could only lift me temporarily. I woke up crying again the very next morning—but this time not in gratitude. For some reason, I felt restless in my spirit.

Later that day I heard from Pat that his night did not go well after a fight broke out between inmates. Though he had avoided the incident, guards moved him to a different floor at 3 a.m. This change made Pat uneasy since he had felt safe around the men on the other floor.

Within a few days, Pat learned that every inmate on his previous floor had to be chained to one another whenever they left for meals or for any other reason. They also lost their phone privileges.

Once again, we saw God's protection over Pat.

The next weekend, Alan and Alix drove from Austin to spend time with Andrew and me. This family time helped to soothe my anxious state, especially when we attended church together on Sunday.

As our pastor preached from John 13, I made notes in my journal, as usual, to record insights. First, I noted that Jesus mourned the state of the world, not just the actions of Judas, who would betray him. Then I wrote that Satan hoped to get the glory by working through Judas; yet his power is restricted since he does not know the future.

I needed to remember that God is sovereign and He alone knows the outcome of our circumstances. But the future—the unknown—still terrified me. While I tried to dispel my fears as soon as they hit me, I too often went to bed in fear and woke up in fear.

The most ordinary events unnerved me, like the hot water heater leak in late July, followed by the air conditioner going out. Around the same time, a small electrical fire started in Andrew's bathroom fan unit. Though nothing flooded or burned, these small events weakened my spirit.

Unsettling global events also came one after another in those last weeks of summer. Conflict in the Middle East escalated, Ebola erupted in West Africa, a Malaysian airliner crashed over Ukraine (possibly by missile assault), and ISIS forces attacked Christians in Iran. This barrage of distressing world news added to my anxiety.

When a friend gave me the book *Cry of the Soul*, I gained comfort from insights as I battled fear:

> Fear distorts our perception of ourselves so that we seem weaker than we really are. It distorts the size of our problems so they seem huge and undefeatable . . . Fear reverses reality by making evil seem all-conquering and God impotent.[1]

Two prayer efforts initiated by Dee Dee further served to allay my fears. First, she set up a monthly prayer calendar so our friends and family could select specific days to pray for us. She also sent our prayer team a daily guide she compiled, calling it "Forty Days of Prayer through the Psalms."

The prayer guide, which I printed and mailed to Pat, included psalms of lament that reveal the psalmist's anguish before he transitions to praise as he recalls God's abundant love and help. Each of the forty selected psalms spoke clearly to our situation.

Three days into this prayer effort, Andrew received and accepted a job offer from the company he interned with that summer. The full-time job would begin in January, after his graduation. Pat and I could anticipate Andrew's return to San Antonio to begin his career—a huge relief.

On day ten of praying through the psalms, Andrew and I discovered over breakfast that we both awoke at 4 a.m., even though our bedrooms were at opposite sides of the house. We thought this strange since neither of us heard anything to cause us to wake. But we found meaning through a phone call the next day.

"You have a prepaid call from an inmate at a federal prison. Will you accept?"

"Yes!"

"Luann, I'm in the federal camp in Bastrop. I'm sorry I couldn't call you sooner, but they woke me at 4 a.m. yesterday, and I didn't arrive here until 9:30 last night. The good news is that I think you can come visit me this weekend."

I cried in relief at the thought of seeing Pat after so long. But it pained me to think he'd endured a seventeen-hour transit—with shackled wrists and ankles—for what should have been a two-hour trip.

The psalm reading that day included our "battle cry," Psalm 18:2: "The Lord is my rock, my fortress and my deliverer; my God is my rock, in whom I take refuge."

I shared the happy news with Alan, who, not knowing a visit would be possible, had already made plans to celebrate his first wedding anniversary with Alix. However, since Bastrop is much closer to Austin, Alan could make the short drive to visit his dad the following weekend.

I waited with excitement for Andrew to get home from work before telling him we could see his dad soon. My son had a surprise for me as well. He had purchased the book *You'll Get Through This*, by the well-known pastor and author Max Lucado. On the inside cover, Andrew had written these words:

> *I know days are tough and everything seems to be a struggle, but I promise you God will never leave your side. We will fight this fight together with God in our corner reminding us just to keep the faith. God would not test you if he didn't think you could handle it.*
>
> *We as a family are a testament to everyone who has faced trials in their lives. If they see that we praise God in this storm, then people will see just how far faith goes. Trust me, God is hurting right now. More than we are. He was also hurting when Jesus was on the cross. But no matter the struggle or the attempts by Satan, one lesson that each follower in the Bible comes to realize is that you'll get through this.*

My tears—always on the ready these days—were now joyful ones. Knowing that Andrew recognized the source of our strength encouraged me more than his job offer.

Andrew was getting through this. Alan and Alix had each other. And Pat had a safer and more comfortable setting. My family's well-being made me feel more secure and less fearful.

After three days of waiting for his visitation privileges to be approved, Pat had not received official notice. Even so, Andrew and I decided on faith to make the two-hour trip to visit him that first Sunday.

We had church in the car that morning by choosing another sermon podcast and praying together. After we asked God to grant us visitation privileges, the phone rang.

"Luann! You and Andrew can come today."

"That's good—because we will be there in fifteen minutes!"

As Pat stepped into the visitation room, a mix of emotions overwhelmed all three of us. Seeing him in the government-issued green uniform brought me to tears. We noticed his ashen face and dramatic weight loss; yet, hugging him after our thirty-three-day separation felt oh-so-wonderful.

It was a relief to cry together instead of apart and to feel Pat's hand tenderly wipe away my tears. In that first embrace I experienced the words I'd read that morning from our psalm of the day: "he restores my soul" (Psalm 23:3).

For the entire four-hour visit in the overcrowded, noisy space, I held my husband's arm as a frightened child might cling to a parent. Meanwhile, Andrew tried to inject normal conversation into the awful circumstances. When visitation ended, our son's bravery kept me from crumbling in front of his dad. Pat checked in with the guard before entering the restricted area behind closed doors. Andrew and I solemnly walked to my car—where I could safely crumble.

Pat received distressing news only two days later. Unaware of phone-use restrictions at the facility, he had used nearly an entire month's allotment of minutes in the first six days. His remaining fifty minutes needed to last through the rest of August—eighteen more days.

Though we mourned the loss of daily conversation, we could e-mail each other for the first time. Now, instead of taking time to pray with me at the end of his brief call, Pat typed and sent his prayer each evening for me to read before bed.

In turn, I e-mailed Pat each morning to share my devotional reading and Scripture passage for the day, along with notes on how God had spoken to me through them. This new routine included anxious waiting for his reply since the correctional system had a two-hour delay for e-mail transmissions.

Though I felt blessed by our communications, nothing was easy. Like the phone minutes, Pat's daily computer time also was limited. And I was uncomfortable knowing that prison officials screened all e-mail, phone calls, and letters. I prayed for God to pierce the heart of anyone reading or listening to our words—that His Word would touch that person.

Andrew and I read Pat's prayers together each night, and we continued to pray with one another at bedtime, which we'd done since Pat's first phone call from lockdown. I cherished this time together, especially knowing it would soon end with his return to college for his last semester.

I wondered how I would manage living alone for the first time in my life. At least I would still have Ellie Mae for a companion, though her stress level seemed to match mine—she'd begun licking the walls several times a day.

Around 9:45 p.m. on my first night alone, the phone rang: Andrew.

"Mom, I know nights are hard on you, and I want you to know that I will call you every night to pray with you. Is now a good time?"

In the morning, the phone rang again: Alan.

"Mom, I know it's hard on you since Andrew left for college. I'll call you every morning and evening just to make sure you're OK."

It comforted me to know my sons were committed to praying for us. And I knew other family members as well as many friends were doing the same.

Patti also called often to check on me, and she continued to send encouraging words. Soon after Andrew left, she shared a message by the well-known pastor Louie Giglio. The heart of that message was this: Embrace the darkness; God is in it. When God's people are wounded greatly, they are used greatly.

These words struck me as something new to consider. Yet I could not imagine how our ordeal could benefit anyone else.

The week after my first visit with Pat, I stopped at the dry cleaners. Maribel saw me coming and handed me a card that contained a two-inch-square cellophane bag.

"Do you know what is in this bag?" She waited eagerly for my response.

"It looks like ashes," I answered.

Maribel explained she'd written the names of both the prosecutor and the judge on a piece of paper and prayed over them for several weeks. Then, deciding it was "time to forgive and release them," she burned the paper and put the ashes in the bag. On the card she wrote words from Isaiah 61:3: "to bestow on them a crown of beauty instead of ashes."

I welcomed Maribel's symbolic offering as a tangible reminder to forgive our enemies, knowing this would be a vital part of our restoration. When I turned to leave the cleaners, another woman arrived, and Maribel began jumping up and down in surprise.

"Luann! Luann! This is the woman I told you about. She has the oil for you."

Two months earlier—a few weeks before Pat left us—Maribel wrote our names on a piece of paper and gave it to a friend who planned to visit Jerusalem. She asked the woman to place the paper between the ancient stones of the Wailing Wall.

Instead, Maribel's friend decided to put our names in the Garden of Gethsemane. She did this on the ninth of July without any knowledge of the significant timing: Pat reported to prison the same day and ended up in solitary confinement by evening. On the darkest day of Pat's life, this woman we didn't know had placed his name at the scene of our Lord's darkest hours. In that same garden on the Mount of Olives, Jesus had cried out, "Father, if you are willing, take this cup from me; yet not my will, but yours be done" (Luke 22:42).

Maribel's friend also brought back olive oil for Pat and me from the trees of that hallowed garden. I left the dry cleaners that day with the oil and the ashes.

Back home, I looked up the verse Maribel had given me with the bag of ashes. As I continued reading the remaining words of Isaiah 61:3, which Maribel hadn't included on her card, the message jumped out at me: " . . . the oil of gladness instead of mourning, and a garment of praise instead of a spirit of despair." Now I was truly amazed to have the oil to go with my ashes!

I also read another passage of Scripture that validated Maribel's unusual act:

Do not take revenge, my friends, but leave room for God's wrath, for it is written: "It is mine to avenge; I will repay," says the Lord. On the contrary: "If your enemy is hungry, feed him; if he is thirsty, give him something to drink. In doing this, you will heap burning coals on his head" (Romans 12:19, 20).

I wanted to be free of my bitterness and at peace in the knowledge of God's ability to avenge wrong. At least Maribel's ashes could serve to remind me to leave our enemies in His hands.

I poured some of the Garden of Gethsemane oil into a tiny plastic vial to take with me to Bastrop the next day. I couldn't wait to tell Pat the significance of the oil and ashes.

During this second visit, I removed the vial from the prison-approved clear pencil pouch that held my keys and some cash for vending machines. Pat and I anointed each other's hands with the oil and thanked God for His presence and provision. This small but meaningful act became our habit on every visit.

Pat gained encouragement through a bounty of mail he received in his first week at Bastrop. More than twenty friends had written caring letters to let him know they were praying. But his stack of mail also made him feel sorry for other inmates who had little support from family and friends. They had never seen anyone get as much mail as Pat. Some of these men shared their heartrending stories with Pat. His concern for them resulted in another habit for future visits. We began to pray for each one by name.

Besides the support of writing letters, Pat's friends soon began to do more. Mitch had taken the lead in a visitation effort by creating a spreadsheet that included many of Pat's close friends. A total of nineteen men signed up for Saturday visits to the prison camp on a rotating schedule.

Pat's brothers and his sister-in-law, as well as my sister and brother-in-law, also began making regular trips to see him. His mother, Linda, faithfully drove alone to Bastrop from her Houston suburb of Pasadena, a nearly three-hour trip. At age seventy-four, she displayed the same resilience of spirit we saw in her after Pat's father died.

Psalm 31:7 says, "I will be glad and rejoice in your love, for you saw my affliction and knew the anguish of my soul."

In this worst season of our lives, Pat and I could sense God's presence. All the love and reassurance we received through every kind word and deed of those who ministered to us in so many ways seemed to come straight from the hand of God.

# Chapter 9

# When God Speaks

*For there is a proper time and procedure
for every matter, though a man's
misery weighs heavily upon him.*

ECCLESIASTES 8:6

In his second week at Bastrop, Pat attended a worship service and heard another sermon about Nicodemus. This was the same topic as the one-on-one Bible study his first evening at the Bexar County facility. Was this a coincidence?

I searched for other scriptures about Nicodemus, who was a Pharisee, a member of the Jewish council, and a secret believer in Jesus. What I found amazed me because of Pat's unjust circumstances. John 7:50, 51 says, "Nicodemus, who had gone to Jesus earlier and who was one of their own number, asked, 'Does our law condemn anyone without first hearing him to find out what he is doing?'"

Then I read my Bible's commentary on that verse: "Pride

would interfere with their ability to reason. . . . What was good and right no longer mattered."[1] It further explained that when Nicodemus confronted the Pharisees about keeping their laws regarding justice, his question exposed their wrong motives, which made them take measures to protect themselves.

I cried as I read the words of that commentary but also thanked God for using them to speak to me. Pat and I believed the prosecutor's desire for a successful outcome had trumped justice in Pat's case so that what was "good and right" did not matter.

While Pat appreciated the worship services at Bastrop, I gleaned encouragement from the book Andrew had given me, *You'll Get Through This.* Max Lucado's account of Joseph's betrayal by his brothers spoke clearly to me and addressed my fear of evil: "[God] allows Satan to unleash mayhem, but He doesn't allow Satan to triumph."[2]

Lucado also mentioned the question that continually plagued me: Who was to blame? His answer included the same scripture that Larry—my Jesus-with-skin-on—gave me at the bookstore three years earlier, shortly after Pat's indictment. Lucado offered John 9:3: "'Neither this man nor his parents sinned,' said Jesus, 'but this happened so that the work of God might be displayed in his life.'"

"God turned blindness, a bad thing, into a billboard for Jesus' power to heal," Lucado writes. "Satan acted, God counteracted, and good won. It's a divine jujitsu of sorts. . . . He is the master chess player, always checkmating the devil's moves."[3]

God was speaking directly to Pat with the repetition of

Nicodemus, and He was speaking directly to me with the repetition of the story with Jesus and the blind man.

I began to e-mail Pat excerpts from each day's reading in Lucado's book. Then one morning in my prayer time, after deciding Pat needed his own copy, I felt God speak to me: *Pat does need this book, but so do many other men at Bastrop.* A sort-of "conversation" followed.

*Yes, Father, I agree with you, but how could I send books to so many?*

*You can't, but you have friends who would love to help out, and they could not only send books but serve as prayer warriors for the men they buy the books for.*

*OK, I will ask Pat the next time I talk to him, and maybe he can start a Bible study.*

*Now, you're thinking.*

Pat liked that idea and mentioned it to a few men he thought might want to read the book as part of a Bible study. The number of those interested soon grew to nineteen!

Following the suggestion that I believed the Lord had provided, I e-mailed nineteen friends from church and the neighborhood to explain how they could help. Just twenty-one days after that morning talk with God, each of the nineteen inmates had received his own book—all through God's provision and timing!

Besides our spiritual encouragement, we received positive updates from Nancy about the appeal process. She apologized for the delays but explained how they allowed her more time to gain insight and information to strengthen Pat's appeal.

We told ourselves not to let the delays disappoint us but to trust God's timing. Even so, we both struggled on a daily basis, tossed by waves of anguish over the injustice of it all.

Toward the end of August, I could tell Pat's positive outlook was waning. Though he tried to hide his misery, I could see the strain in his face from the moment he entered the visiting room. And the sweltering summer heat wasn't helping his low spirits.

In our conversation, he mentioned he hadn't seen a cardinal since leaving home and how he missed this reassuring sign of God's presence. We agreed, however, that God was with us, whether we had visible signs or not.

A few minutes later I left Pat sitting at the outdoor picnic table while I went to get bottled water from a vending machine. When I returned, he had a brighter countenance.

"Luann, turn around and look right behind you."

A beautiful red cardinal stood on the ground only several feet away. The bird stayed a few moments longer, as if waiting to be sure we didn't miss his visit.

We certainly did not miss experiencing God's presence that day.

Despite so many assurances—Scriptures, books, cardinals, and more—my spirit still churned within me. I related so strongly to King David, who experienced emotional turmoil and poured out his heart to God in psalms.

While praying through Psalm 69 as part of our "Forty Days in the Psalms," I noticed our name in verse 14: "Rescue us from the mire." Our name, Mire, is spelled the same, although it is pronounced "mere." But the word in this verse intrigued me because I hadn't noticed it before.

In a word search of "mire," I learned the noun form means a "disadvantageous or difficult situation," and the verb form means "to hinder, entrap or entangle." We were living the meaning of our name!

Those definitions fit my "sackcloth and ashes" state of mind. I definitely felt hindered and trapped. And depressed! Several well-known causes of circumstantial depression had descended on me, one after another: the deaths of family members, imprisonment of a loved one, marital separation, financial stress.

How could I make sense of the evil that had overtaken our lives? How could I forgive those who hurt us? I continually asked God how to fight this battle.

Along with universal questions that arise in times of trouble, I asked God a specific one that required a clear answer. I needed to know His will regarding sharing the story of our shattered lives: "Father, do you want me to write our story?"

I determined to wait for His answer without telling anyone about the prayer.

The next day I found myself reading the Old Testament book of Habakkuk. It wasn't my go-to reference book. And it wasn't part of my scheduled Bible reading for the day. The book begins with the prophet complaining to God: "Why do you make me look at injustice? Why do you tolerate wrong? . . . The wicked hem in the righteous, so that justice is perverted" (Habakkuk 1:3, 4).

The Lord's reply to Habakkuk in the next chapter pronounces coming judgment on the evildoers, and then He assures the prophet: "Though it linger, wait for it; it will certainly come and will not delay" (Habakkuk 2:3). But first, God told him to do something right away to serve as a permanent testimony of His mighty acts. Verse two says, "Write down the revelation and make it plain on tablets so that a herald may run with it."

I made note of that verse in my journal, thinking it had significance regarding my prayer about writing a book.

Toward evening, a friend stopped by to encourage me. Before leaving, Patricia stood on the front porch and asked, "You are writing a book, right? Your story would reach people." Her out-of-the-blue question surprised me, though I only smiled in response. I believed this was a second affirmation regarding a possible book.

Later in the evening, another friend sent me information I'd requested. She ended her message with a strange remark: "You could use this in Pat's book." Her random comment amazed me.

But I needed further clarification, and the Lord soon used Patti to supply it. In her call the next morning, Patti spoke totally off the subject, without my mentioning the comments of my friends the previous day. "I won't let you not write a book," she said.

I knew these unsolicited encouragements—three of them—provided an answer to my prayer, but this realization produced a new dilemma in short order. My mind and emotions remained in a vortex, which drained me. I was in no shape to write a book unless God would energize me and help me organize my thoughts.

Ready or not, I said yes to God. I would write our story. But I knew it wouldn't be a "how-to" book; I still didn't know how to get through this! Instead, I would write a "yes-to" book: yes to trusting God in uncertainty; yes to surrendering to His purposes; and yes to glorifying God in suffering.

On one of my visits with Pat, we realized our conversations often depressed us. Since I had begun the habit of recording ten blessings in my journal each week, we decided to do the same during our visits. And we determined to look for tangible rather than vague encouragements.

Still in the throes of the blistering August heat, we had to look hard for those blessings. During one visit we realized we killed only three bees instead of the ten we had to smash the week before. This "blessing" made the list.

Our stretching to find blessings kept us focused on small victories instead of the concerns of our larger battle. This habit also helped me shed the sackcloth that threatened to suffocate me.

Further, I needed to dust off the ashes, especially since Patti planned to drive down from Dallas the following week. She and I had scheduled three days together to organize my writing project—only four weeks after I first sought God's will about a book!

I had many reasons to dread the long and difficult task of telling our story. However, I hoped that looking back through my journals and recalling everything God had done so far would give me fresh courage for whatever lay ahead.

I referred to my journals as my "Ebenezer." The name comes from the time when the prophet Samuel erected a stone as a memorial of God's past victories: "He named it Ebenezer, saying, 'Thus far has the Lord helped us'" (1 Samuel 7:12).

A few hours after Patti arrived from Dallas, Maribel texted me to say she felt the Lord calling her to a three-day fast on my behalf. And she had no idea about my writing project or Patti's visit!

What could I say to Maribel's faithfulness? I thanked her, and I thanked God for her and for this further confirmation of His guidance for my writing.

I felt overjoyed to see Patti again, even though we had talked by phone several times a week since Pat left. But a flare-up of pain in my jaw during her visit seemed determined to hinder our conversations and the writing sessions she had planned.

The unrelenting pain began shortly before Pat left. The emotional anguish at that time and all the crying that went with it affected my jaw. I had difficulty opening my mouth wide enough to eat or speak properly. Taking pain-relief medicine every four hours only lessened the discomfort. My aching jaw affected my entire body and added to my fragile emotions.

On the second morning of Patti's visit, I woke exhausted and feeling discouraged. The writing task seemed too heart-wrenching and difficult to attempt. I couldn't hide my fears from Patti.

"Why would anyone want to read my story? It's too painful."

Patti observed my distressed face and slumped posture while she listened to my anxious words.

"Let's push our writing session back and spend more time in God's Word and prayer this morning," she suggested.

We sat down with our Bibles and coffee and looked at my place of reading for that day, Isaiah 43:19: "See, I am doing a new thing! Now it springs up; do you not perceive it? I am making a way in the desert and streams in the wasteland."

Reading that verse reminded me of words I'd come across recently. I picked up my copy of *Beautiful Battle* to find the passage and read it to Patti: "God's about to do amazing things, creating pathways through our wilderness lives and waterways through our parched souls, but if we continue to look back with longing for what was, we could miss the things God is doing today. To pine for the glory years is to give Satan a foothold on your attitude."[4]

I still looked back with longing for the days before injustice overtook our lives. My life had become a wilderness existence. But reading these words made me realize I didn't want to miss whatever God had in mind.

As we closed our time in God's Word, Patti and I prayed that He would use my family's circumstances to do "a new thing."

When we headed down the hall to my office for our writing session, I received a text from Marthe, the friend who had come to our house to pray room by room. She had no idea I felt like giving up the book project before it even began, but still, she sent the words of Ecclesiastes 8:6: "For there is a time and a way for everything, although man's trouble lies heavy on him" (ESV). This message affirmed and energized me.

Patti and I made substantial progress that day as we constructed a detailed outline. My story was taking shape!

Our three days together seemed blessed, and we thanked God for His help and for Maribel's fasting. We both felt strengthened by the power of her prayers.

After Patti left for Dallas, I picked up a smoothie for Maribel, knowing her fast was over. She was excited to see me, anxious to share the words she felt the Lord gave her during her prayer time. She said He spoke to her spirit the words "water" and "honor" concerning Pat. Maribel said Pat is like water in a desert to all who know him, whether here or in Bastrop, that he is a man of honor, and that his honor would be restored.

Back home, teary-eyed from the blessing of Maribel's words, I picked up the day's mail and opened a letter from Pat. The envelope included a letter Patti's husband, Jim, sent to Pat several weeks earlier. Jim's words were so meaningful that Pat wanted to share them with me.

I opened the letter right away and became overwhelmed with emotion at receiving a second message about water and honor. Jim wrote:

> *I want to share some things I believe the Lord showed me while praying for you when you were first imprisoned. Call it a vision or perhaps my mind's eye, but I saw a huge rock, and it was split open. The inside had a hollow core with what looked like pearl lining. As I looked closer, the core was filled with water—pure, refreshing, and restoring. I began praying, "Split the rock, Lord, split the rock."*
>
> *I have prayed this prayer many times for you since then, and I encourage you to pray the same when you need to "drink" from that reservoir. I believe there is a wellspring prepared specifically for you, to sustain you.*
>
> *Psalm 105:39-41 talks of God's provision when the Israelites left Egypt: "He spread out a cloud as a covering, and a fire to give light at night. They asked, and he brought them quail and satisfied them with the bread of heaven. He opened the rock, and water gushed out; like a river it flowed in the desert."*
>
> *The second thing that came to me, which seems so contrary to your circumstances, but I believe to be true, is that God has placed you in a place of "honor." How your current residence can be called a place of honor I can't understand, but I know that if we honor God in all of our circumstances, He will bring forth his perfect plan.*
>
> *With "restoring water" and a "seat of honor," you are in good Hands.*

I cried at this repetition of inspired words. I couldn't fathom that the God of the universe would reach down to reveal Himself to me. I had to believe that God was indeed making a way through the desert for us. Meanwhile, He was providing streams in the wasteland as well.

# Chapter 10

# Divine Delays

*Stand firm and you will see the deliverance the
Lord will bring you today. . . . The Lord will fight
for you; you need only to be still.*

EXODUS 14:13, 14

Driving home from Bastrop the weekend after Patti's visit, I
heard a pastor on the radio say, "If God is in it" you can expect
delays. His words referenced 2 Peter 3:9, which says, "The
Lord is not slow in keeping his promise, as some understand
slowness."

Later in the week I read a similar message in Mark
Buchanan's book *Your God Is Too Safe*: "Prayer and waiting
are intrinsically linked, joined at the hip. . . . So it is vital—
not merely an academic concern, but a burning one—that we
grasp the logic of divine delay." Buchanan also writes: "Prayer
is just that: crying out day and night without seeing justice
and continuing anyhow. . . . To pray well is to cultivate holy

patience and perseverance."[1]

Oh, how we had seen delays as we prayed and waited for the appeal to be filed. Meanwhile, issues at home did not delay. Our appliances did not know Pat was away!

When the light on our icemaker blinked incessantly to remind me it needed cleaning, I texted Dee Dee to ask if her husband, Perry, could stop by to work on it. Several days went by without hearing back from her, which seemed strange. But then Perry called.

"Luann, Dee Dee and I want to take you to dinner tonight."

"Oh, I'm guessing you saw my text regarding the icemaker?"

"No, I don't know anything about that," Perry said. "But I'll check it when we pick you up for dinner."

Later that evening, while Perry worked on the refrigerator, Dee Dee checked her phone and realized my texts to her had been blocked, though she had no idea how to block texts or why this happened to my texts.

Before they left that night, Dee Dee expressed concern, asking if I had any specific prayer needs. I hesitated before telling her about the continual pain and tension in my jaw. After we sat at the kitchen table, she placed her hands on my right jaw and began to pray. Immediately, I felt a tingling sensation coursing through my jaw, ear, and down my neck.

Afterward, I opened my mouth without feeling any pain or tenderness. I went to bed later without needing to take medicine, and I slept through the night without pain. I had never experienced a healing like this, and I knew it wasn't my imagination!

When I called Dee Dee the next morning to share the good news, we thanked God together. Those "blocked" texts on her phone were no match for God, who supersedes the airwaves.

Patti also rejoiced to hear my news. Having witnessed my

pain during the three days of her visit, she had begun praying daily for my healing. And, unknown to me, she had asked her Bible study group to pray specifically for my jaw.

My healed jaw improved my perspective on nearly everything. I could enjoy eating and speaking normally again. All to the glory of God!

With each visit to Bastrop, Alan and Andrew saw their dad's positive influence on other inmates. They watched as visitors came over to thank Pat for making the Lucado book available for a Bible study. Our sons also met several men, young and old, who stopped at our table to say how Pat went out of his way to help them. Alan and Andrew weren't surprised; they knew their dad—always giving himself to others.

But all three of us were surprised when Pat said the number of men interested in the Bible study had grown to thirty-eight! Each of the nineteen men who received a book would share with another man, which would give them an accountability partner in the process.

I felt so blessed that the men's Bible study originated from a single event: Andrew's sudden stop at a bookstore to encourage me. My son continued to comfort me after his return to college. In one call he said, "Mom, we are doing all that we can. We are obeying God. He will bless our obedience."

The next day I read these words from a book on prayer by E.M. Bounds: "God cannot help hearing the prayer of an obedient child."[2]

I observed a growing faith in both my sons as our trials continued. And, as they expressed their trust in God, my faith grew stronger.

Pat continued to e-mail his prayers to me each night. On one occasion, he wrote a psalm-like poem as a prayer.

*I sit here in this exile,*
*Where evil worlds collide.*
*But Lord, You're with my family,*
*I know You will provide.*

*Our outer man's decaying;*
*This world can be so cold.*
*Our inner man's pure spirit*
*Is joyful to the soul.*

*But worldly aspirations*
*Show temporal things we see.*
*Our God says look toward Him—*
*Find eternal life with Me.*

*We plan our lives so carefully,*
*Not knowing where we stand.*
*But our great Lord and Savior*
*Controls the long-term plan.*

The Lord refreshed me through Pat's prayers and poems in the same way He strengthened me during my quiet time with Him. My morning devotions included a daily Bible reading plan, and in the week the appeal would be filed, one reading provided "living" words from Isaiah 8:12-14, 16.

Do not call conspiracy everything that these people call conspiracy; do not fear what they fear, and do not dread it. The Lord Almighty is the one you are to regard as holy, he is the one you are to fear, he is the one you are to dread, and he will be a sanctuary. . . . Bind up the testimony.

That word, *conspiracy*, lunged at me, causing me to pay attention to the passage. I was amazed to find three obvious parallels to our situation: the prosecutor had presented Pat to the judge as a coconspirator; Pat and I looked to the Lord Almighty as our sanctuary; and Nancy worked on our behalf to bind up the testimony.

As the appeal deadline approached, I prepared for a mid-October prayer retreat. Bonnie had told me about Ruach Journey months earlier, while Pat was still at home. She knew I had read the retreat director's powerful book, *Blessing Your Spirit.* (I'd actually read it five times and given copies to others!) She and I prayed about attending the conference in Birmingham, Alabama, and then we registered soon after Pat left home.

Part of our conference preparation included study materials. Passages like the following served to prime my heart to hear from God:

When you feel that you're in a wilderness, be blessed to drink from living waters that stream from the hard places because he is your Spiritual Rock (1 Corinthians 10:4). . . . Psalm 107:35 says, "He turned the desert into pools of water and the parched ground into flowing springs." Be blessed with the Fountain of living waters welling up in you. . . . God will make the Valley of Trouble into a place of springs, and you will go from strength to strength in him (Psalm 84:6). Be blessed from his righteous spring of blessing that is flowing to you. Let him fill you up and pour you out to others who are thirsty.[3]

There it was again: Living Water in hard places; parched ground into flowing springs; valley of trouble into a place of springs. God was the only One who could quench my thirst. I prayed for Him to fill me up!

On the first Friday of October, the day we expected the appeal to be filed, I planned to go out for some needed items for our trip. When a friend called to ask if we could meet for lunch, I suggested a restaurant somewhere in the vicinity of my shopping destination—one I rarely visit.

The lunch date would soon appear to be a setup for one of God's divine purposes.

That particular Friday ushered in the Jewish holy day Yom Kippur, and I spent my prayer time reflecting on the spiritual significance of this observance.

I esteem the Jewish faith as the root of my Christian heritage. And knowing Yom Kippur was Nancy's deadline for filing Pat's appeal, I had taken another look at the feast of Rosh Hashanah. This ten-day celebration of new beginnings culminates on Yom Kippur.

God ordained these holy days for His people to offer Him thanks and praise. They begin with blowing the shofar—essentially a ram's horn used as a trumpet blast. The feast days close with Yom Kippur, also referred to as the Day of Atonement, when God's people offered animal sacrifices to atone for their sins. This ritual included a *scapegoat*. According to Leviticus 16:22, "The goat will carry on itself all their sins to a solitary place."

I saw obvious analogies for us. We wanted to "blow the shofar" to celebrate with thanks and praises to God. We recognized God's Son as the one who bore our sins, and we saw Pat as a scapegoat—suffering for the wrongs of others.

I could not ignore the formidable forces against us. Our lives had been shattered by the prosecutor's use of incriminating words. My anxieties always waited in the shadows while we hoped for the wrong to be reversed so our lives would be restored.

Earlier that week, I read an illuminating passage in *God's Prayer Book,* by Ben Patterson: "Only the God of truth can free us from lies. . . . In the final analysis, we are too weak in ourselves to fight against lies. The Lord must fight for us."[4]

Entering the soup and sandwich shop that Friday, I found my friend, Rhonda, waiting at a table she'd selected. I went to place my order at the counter and proceeded to the drink station. Filling my glass with tea, I noticed the man beside me looked familiar.

I don't know how I kept from fainting when I realized who stood just inches from me: the prosecutor. How could it be possible that I would see him on the very day Pat's appeal would be filed? I had not seen him since the sentencing day in February.

I told myself to stand firm, but as I turned to walk to my seat, the last man I wanted to see was sitting at the table next to ours, though he did not appear to see me.

I leaned toward Rhonda to whisper my request to change tables. As we moved to a safer spot, my mind raced with questions. Was the prosecutor discussing Pat's appeal with those at his table? Why did he come to this restaurant on this day and at this time?

When I explained my sudden anxiety, my friend said we could leave. But I only wanted her to pray for my strength. I also prayed for this very man in my presence. Afterward, I somehow ate my lunch.

That disturbing incident gnawed at me for the rest of the day. I reasoned that it couldn't be by chance. I wondered about the possible significance, but had no answer. I trusted that God had a reason.

The next morning, Saturday, I planned to pick up Alan and Andrew in Austin so we could visit Pat together. Before leaving, I reached for Patterson's devotional book. At a glance of the day's reading, Psalm 23, I thought the familiar psalm would offer nothing particularly new for this morning. But as I came to verse five, I began to sob because of the fresh meaning of the words: "You prepare a table before me in the presence of my enemies."

After my initial shock, I went on to read Patterson's comments: "Praise God for the decisive defeat of your enemies. . . . God will be victorious; he will vindicate his chosen one."[5] The author further described what I had experienced at the sandwich shop. He explained that no matter how good the food may be, dining in the presence of your enemy is not appealing; digestion might even be a problem.

The Creator of all Heaven and earth was involved in our personal lives, all the way to preparing a table for me in the presence of my enemy. I couldn't wait to share the past twenty-four hours with Pat and the boys that day.

When Pat heard the story during our visit, he had something to add to the events of the previous day. He shared Nancy's latest message. She had filed the appeal on Friday evening around eight o'clock.

Pat," I exclaimed. "That means it was filed at sunset—the eve of Yom Kippur."

# Chapter 11

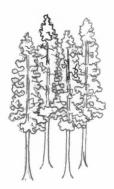

# Renowned in Battle

*Though an army besiege me, my heart will not fear. . . . For in the day of trouble he will keep me safe in his dwelling.*

PSALM 27:3, 5

Settling into the routine of driving to Bastrop every Sunday provided some structure to the void in my life, but it didn't allow me to worship at our church on Sunday mornings. I needed to find a church that offered other worship times.

On the Sunday evening after the appeal was filed, I asked Vicki to go with me to a service at a nearby church. It felt so good to be in God's house, even if I didn't know anyone in the congregation. Still, the believers around me seemed like family.

The service began with a song that struck me as more than coincidental. We sang the words from 2 Samuel 22:1, 2 that Pat and I had coined as our battle cry: *Praise the name of Jesus. He's my rock, He's my fortress, He's my deliverer; in Him will I trust.*

After the time of worship, the young pastor gave a short sermon before closing with a prayer, Saint Patrick's "Lorica":

Against the demon snares of sin,
The vice that gives temptation force,
The natural lusts that war within,
The hostile men that mar my course;
Or few or many, far or nigh,
In every place and in all hours,
Against their fierce hostility
I bind to me those holy powers.

Against all Satan's spells and wiles,
Against false words of heresy,
Against the knowledge that defiles,
Against the heart's idolatry,
Against the wizard's evil craft,
Against the death wound and the burning,
The choking wave, the poisoned shaft,
Protect me, Christ, till Thy returning.[1]

Pat was born the day after St. Patrick's Day and named for this saint, but I had never heard that prayer. And it was much later that I learned the meaning of the word *lorica*, which is Latin for "body armor." Yet on this evening, the stark correlation of the words to our situation pierced me—God had my attention. Between the opening "battle cry" and this classic prayer for divine protection, I felt poised for battle—without knowing what the next day would hold.

"Luann, I have to come to San Antonio tomorrow for a deposition in November." Pat was upset. "They want me to answer a few questions in front of a judge."

"I don't understand. November is four weeks away!"

We had known Pat might be called upon to provide statements about one of the companies involved in his case. But why did he need to return to the jail facility where we could not visit him?

I had looked forward—perhaps selfishly—to leaving for the retreat in two days. I needed a break from the barrage of evil we faced. But now my attention was entirely diverted to Pat's trip, especially as I recalled his previous "two-hour transit" that took seventeen hours.

However, I needed to remind myself of God's provision in the past forty-eight hours. He had prepared a table before me in the presence of our enemy, orchestrated our battle cry during the church service, and thrown in a prayer for protection courtesy of Saint Patrick.

After Pat's disturbing call, I read a timely comment on Psalm 27: "If you are beset and besieged, and would love to see God bring his big fist down on the heads of the enemies of your soul, this is your psalm. Ask the Lord to make you eagerly and expectantly patient."[2]

Psalm 27:13, 14 says, "I am still confident of this: I will see the goodness of the Lord in the land of the living. Wait for the Lord; be strong and take heart and wait for the Lord."

I didn't know how to reconcile eager expectancy with patience, but I asked the Lord to help me.

Since Pat's transfer was delayed twenty-four hours, he actually left for San Antonio the same day I flew to Alabama. One thought gave me solace. I considered that perhaps God was removing Pat from trouble.

A new warden had arrived in Bastrop only the week before,

and in that short time her cruel treatment of the inmates intimidated them. First, she ordered that all picnic tables be chained together, which restricted privacy during family visits. She then overreacted to an elderly asthmatic inmate who had requested another job in place of cleaning bathrooms because of the harsh-smelling chemicals. Instead of considering his health, she severely punished him, ordering the poor man to stay in an unventilated supply closet where he would have to breathe those same fumes for several hours.

I tried to pray both for this woman and the men who suffered from her irrational demands. At least Pat was away from her for now. Maybe the timing of the deposition was God's provision.

Arriving at the retreat center on Wednesday, Bonnie and I took our boxed lunches outside to enjoy the crisp fall air. We walked down to a lake nestled in pine trees—the area felt like a fortress. The surroundings and scent of the trees stirred fond memories of my college days with Pat since we first met in the Piney Woods region of East Texas . . .

Ironically, I had known Pat's father, who worked as a vice president of the bank in Deer Park where I worked part-time while in high school. Mr. Mire's gentle manner and genuine concern for everyone impressed me. Though I didn't know anything about his family, I once told my mother that I wanted to marry someone just like Mr. Mire, someone who had all of his qualities.

In May of my senior year, despite the dorm deposit my parents had paid to the University of Texas in Austin, I made a sudden decision to attend Stephen F. Austin State University, in Nacogdoches, three hours north of Houston. My parents and one grandmother all graduated from this college.

When Mr. Mire heard of my decision, he told me his son Pat planned to attend SFA also. Sure enough, I met Pat in my biology class that first fall semester. I called home to fill in my mother. "Mr. Mire's son is so nice, and he walked me to my gym class," I said. Mom later said she knew something had changed when I started calling him Pat.

Pat and I dated for more than three years and married soon after our graduation. He proved to be the husband I had hoped for—like father, like son. . . .

Now I felt fresh pangs from the loss of both of my parents and Pat's dad, "Poppy." This, along with missing Pat so intensely, made me wonder how I could bear this setting for three days. I asked God to hold me together and tend to my wounds so I could expectantly see what the retreat would offer.

Day two included a special prayer time with a naming exercise. The leader explained how the planning team had researched the origins of our names and then prayed over them during the month before the retreat. In addition, they had asked God to supply a specific Bible verse for each person.

After receiving the 5x7 piece of parchment paper someone handed me, I couldn't question the validity of the exercise. I gazed wide-eyed at the inscription chosen for me: "Luann, Renowned in Battle." Unbelievable!

But I also wondered: why couldn't mine have said "Beloved Daughter" or "Child of the King"?

Even more amazing, I saw something else. My inscription

included Exodus 15:1, 2, 11, and 13:

*Luann: Renowned in Battle*
*I will sing to the Lord for he is highly exalted.*
*The Lord is my strength and my defense;*
*He is my God, and I will praise him. Who is like you, Lord—*
*Majestic in holiness, awesome in glory, working wonders?*
*In your unfailing love you will lead the people you have*
*redeemed.*

The word *defense* leaped off the parchment. The Lord is my Defender! The verses echoed the words of our battle cry from 2 Samuel 22:1, 2. And both of the Bible passages referred to songs of victory.

I later returned to the pine fortress to read all of Exodus 15, the account of God leading Israel out of Egypt by Moses. Some of the words were more familiar to me because of a popular Chris Tomlin song. There beside the lake I began to sing aloud for the first time since Pat left home: "*Who is like you—majestic in holiness, awesome in glory, working wonders* . . . " I felt as if God was leading me out of my Egypt and healing my wounds.

I'd like to say that God's peace remained upon me, but it vanished in a flash when Pat called that evening. His voice sounded strained.

"Luann, I'm in solitary confinement, and I only have a few minutes to talk."

"Pat! What happened? Why?" I began sobbing.

"It's for my safety. I'll explain later."

How could this happen—again! How could Pat be back in solitary confinement, with no visitation or other basic privileges? How much more of this could he endure?

After I returned home from Birmingham the following day, Pat called a second time and explained the details of his circumstances.

When he arrived at the jail in San Antonio, the same bunk from his August stay was available—good news, since twenty-eight men had to sleep on mats in the chapel due to overcrowding. As he went to bed that first night, an inmate warned him not to sleep there, saying the loud noise of the television on the wall over that bunk would disturb his sleep. But since the only other sleeping option was the floor, Pat said he'd be fine. Within two hours, some inmates called the guard to report that Pat had urinated in their shower and left dirty clothes in the bathroom.

Pat hadn't even left his bunk during the night. False accusations—again!

The guard acquiesced to those accusers by moving Pat to another floor. This new floor looked exceptionally clean, more like a library, with soft lighting and bookshelves that actually included books. His new bunk came with fresh linens—a luxury he didn't have before.

Pat soon learned that the location of his previous bunk served as a "tattoo parlor" of sorts, in which inmates had hot-wired the television to create a stylus for their creative work.

The comforts of Pat's new floor didn't last long. He told his bunkmates he was only there to provide a deposition for the government. This appeared suspect to these inmates, who had their own protocol for dealing with "snitches." The inmates informed Pat he couldn't stay; they didn't welcome a government snitch (another false accusation!). Furthermore, they said, they would beat him to a pulp if he stayed.

A guard responded to the inmates' demand to move Pat but denied their request. However, Pat interjected, not wanting to stay unless the guard would protect him. The guard concluded the only other option was solitary confinement.

At least Pat would be safe!

From his second lockdown circumstance in less than three months, Pat mailed a poem he had written in pencil:

> *I sit here staring*
> *At cold blue bars,*
> *Looking for Jesus*
> *Through so many scars.*
>
> *I know He is with me;*
> *His presence I feel.*
> *But it's hard to see Him*
> *Through so much steel.*
>
> *With this evil around me,*
> *I'll stay in the boat.*
> *But, No, the Lord tells us:*
> *Get out and you'll float.*
>
> *So, I look for my Savior*
> *To help me see clear,*
> *And know when I need Him*
> *He'll always be near.*

In spite of my concerns with Pat's surroundings, I found a reason to be thankful: his awareness of God's presence.

Meanwhile, though my hardships did not compare to Pat's, I had a fresh problem at home. Yellow jackets had taken up residence inside the patio wall. They stung both Ellie Mae and me. A pest control serviceman came and said the bees were the predatory kind. He donned a hazmat suit, mask, and shoe covers to treat the area.

All of our afflictions validated a passage on spiritual warfare I had read by E.M. Bounds: "The average church member today does not seem to know anything about conflict or how the world, the devil, and flesh will try to hinder a believer's walk. There is little or nothing of the soldier element in it. Yet the Christian life is warfare."[3]

Pat and I were learning to embrace the challenges—to "stand the pull." And though I referred to each new difficulty as "a dagger," I also saw how God protected us at each attempted assault. God's Word, especially the psalms, continually supplied us with prayers that fit our circumstances. Psalm 31:4, 5 encouraged me with these words: "Pull me from the trap my enemies set for me, for I find protection in You alone. . . . Rescue me, Lord, for You are a faithful God" (NLT).

We also learned that God's timing does not usually coincide with ours. Pat spent a long week in solitary confinement before he found out—after all his waiting—that the November deposition date was canceled! Instead, he only needed to answer a few questions in the presence of a magistrate, which was good news since the questioning could happen within days. This development seemed like an answer to my prayers for Pat. Though praying for his return to a correctional camp seemed strange.

Four days after Pat received the green light for his transfer back to Bastrop, he remained in solitary confinement. Nancy made inquiries and learned his paperwork had stalled on the desk of a judge on vacation. Ugh! She worked to get another judge to approve Pat's transfer.

At 3:15 the next morning, Pat was awakened and instructed to turn in his bedding and other items he'd been issued and head downstairs to a holding room. After twelve hours of "holding," he was pulled from the group of those awaiting transfer. Due to missing paperwork, a guard escorted him back to solitary confinement.

Though the senseless delay upset me, I hoped God had allowed it for good, to protect Pat. Nancy told me these wrongs could work in his favor, which reminded us of Marion's words: Your afflictions are working for you.

The delay upset me for another reason. My birthday was the following day, and I couldn't enjoy it while my husband was stuck in a system that ran on square wheels. I wanted to spend it with a peaceful heart, knowing Pat had made it safely back to Bastrop.

Pat always made birthdays a special occasion for our family. Days ahead of each of my birthdays he would place gifts on the hearth. Even in these circumstances, Pat—ever faithful—had written a birthday poem for me and mailed it early.

During all of this angst and confusion, God surrounded me with friends. One of them, Jana, came to stay with me that week. Others arranged a birthday gathering for me at a restaurant, complete with flowers and gifts. Despite their love and support, I was a wreck, completely drained. My blood pressure dropped to 80 over 50. And, probably due to my physical condition, my trust in God waned.

The day Jana left, my sister arrived from East Texas for a

visit. Beth and I had grown up making mud pies and sharing clothes, shoes, and later a car—just about everything but contact lenses. Her presence comforted me.

Pat finally returned to Bastrop after twenty-one days in solitary confinement. However, on arrival, he learned that Cruella De Warden was gone from the camp. After receiving a better bunk assignment in a less crowded section, Pat was able to return to his normal routine.

Once again, I saw how God had rescued Pat. I would need Him to rescue me next.

# Chapter 12

# Thankful in All Things

*Get rid of all bitterness, rage and anger.*
EPHESIANS 4:31

Seeing Pat after three weeks was bittersweet. He had lost his regained weight, fifteen pounds worth, from sitting in a six-by-eight-foot cell with no fresh air or sunlight. He looked pale and drained of vitality. But he assured me he was well, and told me the Bastrop inmates, happy to see him again, gave him extra food at mealtimes.

Though I had praised God for Pat's safe return, I found myself in the grip of bitterness. Sylvia Gunter says, "Bitterness is long-held unforgiveness about a wound we received, and unforgiveness hinders prayer. . . . All of life is dysfunctional when seen through the focus of unhealed woundedness."[1]

I needed to forgive Pat's former employer and the judicial system that had wounded us. But how? Someone told me that forgiving hurts can be like weeding a garden. My hurts—like

138

weeds—kept popping up. If I didn't tend to them, they would take over the garden of my soul. However, if I kept after them, I might eventually eradicate them. So I endeavored to "pull weeds" each day during my morning prayer time.

I especially wanted to be free of bitterness for the holidays. Though I had always loved Thanksgiving and Christmas, I now dreaded their approach. How could we celebrate with Pat in prison?

The week before Thanksgiving I grew anxious about my complicated plans to visit Andrew in College Station before we would gather as a family at the Bastrop camp. Then a new arrow hit me—one aimed at Patti.

A biopsy of a spot on the back of Patti's head showed a malignant melanoma. She needed immediate surgery. Thanksgiving week, instead of planning a family gathering, Patti was down with a head wound that resembled the stitching on a football. She was at peace and thankful the cancer had not spread internally, but I was shaken—fearful. In my frail condition, I worried that this faithful friend and source of support might be taken from me.

As Patti and I talked that same week, she shared a Bible passage that got her attention regarding Pat.

> ...in the year Evil-Merodach became king of Babylon, he released Jehoiachin from prison on the twenty-seventh day of the twelfth month. He spoke kindly to him and gave him a seat of honor higher than those of the other kings who were with him in Babylon. So Jehoiachin put aside his prison clothes and for the rest of his life ate regularly at the king's table (2 Kings 25:27-29).

As Patti read the words, my heart jumped. I had noted the same verses in my prayer time earlier the same morning, except I read them in Jeremiah 52:31-34! This obscure passage appears in two books of the Bible, which we had not realized. We'd been reading different books, though neither of us planned to study those books that day. Yet the identical lines stood out to us.

The exiled Israelite king, Jehoiachin, could have died in prison or been treated like a slave upon his release. The account of his freedom on a specific day, and the kind treatment he received—with honor—provided a strong visual image for me. I had been fearful that something or someone would cause Pat to remain at Bastrop longer than expected. Instead, I could prayerfully anticipate that he would certainly come out of prison, perhaps earlier than expected. And he would leave behind that stiff camp uniform. Even more, I could hope that my husband's good reputation would be restored. That word, "honor," especially held meaning!

Thinking about Andrew's December graduation from Texas A&M added to my holiday blues. My son had no desire to participate in his commencement ceremony without his dad. We kept getting robbed of joy!

Perhaps trying to make up for our disappointment, I overscheduled our Thanksgiving week, which began on Wednesday when I drove to College Station with Ellie Mae in the back seat. I would at least be with my son for the annual A&M Thanksgiving Day football game, the last one of his college days.

Andrew and I enjoyed a nice dinner out that first evening, knowing there would be no turkey and dressing for us the next day. Then, with no hotel rooms available the night before the big game, we headed to Andrew's small rental house. He offered to sleep on the den sofa so I could have the privacy of his bedroom.

As I prepared for bed, Andrew proofread the English paper he had worked on all month. I enjoyed seeing the look on his face when he hit the "send" button to turn it in later that night.

Early Thanksgiving morning, the two of us headed to Bastrop, where Alan met us for our family time together. Pat's brother Rod joined us as well. The five of us laughed and somehow enjoyed this strange but tolerable holiday gathering.

On the way back to College Station, Andrew and I stopped at a favorite gas station/convenience store to pick up our Thanksgiving dinner—chicken strips and popcorn. We ate our "feast" in the car as we drove to A&M's new football stadium.

At the game, all I could think of was Pat. He would have enjoyed seeing this impressive stadium and hearing Andrew share his knowledge. I tried to nod with appreciation while Andrew, a construction science major, pointed out the intricate architectural features.

Although Andrew and I enjoyed the game from our seats in the student section, it meant standing the entire time—the tradition at A&M! But all of this standing, after five hours of driving and then walking a mile to and from the stadium, wore me out.

When we returned to Andrew's house, one of his roommates told us his family also could not find a hotel room. They would need to stay overnight—all nine of them. No problem. My six-foot-two-inch son and I could share his bed—with Ellie Mae squeezed between us.

"Be joyful always; pray continually; give thanks in all circumstances, for this is God's will for you in Christ Jesus." I tried hard to hold on to these verses from 1 Thessalonians 5:16-18. They had become commands to me instead of mere suggestions. The words demanded action on my part that required focus and energy, both of which eluded me. I needed God's help.

I drove home on Friday afternoon after very little sleep at Andrew's holiday "hostel." On top of that, the post-Thanksgiving freeway traffic turned my two-hour drive into a grueling four-hour trip. I grew depressed and half desperate at the thought of going home to an empty house. Even though I needed to recoup before returning to Bastrop for my Sunday visit with Pat, I decided to call Vicki and invite myself to dinner. She welcomed me but warned me that her Christmas decorations were spread across the floor. I didn't care.

By Monday, I was drained and bereft of any ability to be joyful, thankful, or prayerful. As multiple concerns pressed in on me, bitterness and anger resurged, and I let them have their way. On the phone with Alan, I expressed my disappointment about Thanksgiving. Ignoring that command in 1 Thessalonians, I instead wallowed in my feelings all day. By evening, my tired and confused mind reasoned that I needed to spend more time with Alan and Alix.

On that dark night, instead of allowing myself more time to recuperate after driving more than sixteen hours in the past five days, I decided to make the trip to Austin. Since I planned to come home later in the evening, I simply grabbed Ellie Mae and headed out into rush-hour traffic—in pouring rain.

During that ninety-mile drive, I called my sister to vent my emotions, but by this point I was beyond reach. Beth must have thought I had lost it! And honestly, I was teetering on the edge.

When I reached Alan's neighborhood, everything looked strange; I had never driven myself there at night. As I circled the area in search of the house, I cried uncontrollably. I called Patti, hoping she would be there to help me calm down. I didn't want my son and daughter-in-law to see me in this condition. Patti was alarmed to hear what I was doing, but she kept me on the phone and prayed with me until I pulled into the right driveway.

I could barely speak when Alan and Alix opened their door. Though they expected me, they must have been shocked at my distraught appearance. Their compassionate welcome made my tears flow again.

This impulsive visit seemed completely irrational, yet being there felt like balm to my weary soul. Instead of returning home later that evening, I agreed to stay overnight. Before bed, Alan said he had a gift for me and handed me a small book with a close-up image of a cardinal on the cover.

"I was saving this for Christmas, Mom. But I decided you need it now."

Alan was right. I wanted to read as soon as I saw the title: *Gift of the Red Bird: The Story of a Divine Encounter.*

The book is a personal account by a woman who, at five months pregnant, lost both her husband and two-year-old daughter in a car accident. To write her story, Paula D'Arcy sought the solitude of a retreat center west of San Antonio—

Laity Lodge!

I felt an instant connection because of that familiar setting. Both Alan and Andrew enjoyed summer camp there in their growing-up years, and during college they returned to serve as camp counselors. I could easily picture the author writing her tragic story with a view of the rocky cliffs and winding riverbed. I couldn't stop reading.

The memoir included the author's faith questions, which I knew too well. *Can I believe when I don't understand?* And: *What is greater, my faith or my fear?*

During D'Arcy's lowest point in her writing, a single cardinal would visit. She explained, "Whenever the red bird appears . . . it is confirmation to me that beyond the material world of cause and effect, there is a dimension of spirit waiting for our recognition."[2]

After reading the entire book, I could barely sleep. However, in place of my bitter, anxious thoughts, I had gratitude. I began to thank God for safe travel to Austin, a warm bed, and Alan's gift.

As December arrived, Pat surprised us with news of preparations for a Christmas pageant at the camp. He explained that a fellow inmate—a former pastor—had written the script. The participants, including Pat, practiced during their weekly Bible study time. He had taken the part of Micah, the Old Testament prophet.

"Micah?" I didn't get it. "I have never heard of a Christmas pageant with Micah in it."

"Yes, Luann," Pat assured me. "Micah is the prophet who told the people that only the Messiah could save them from the tyranny of the day."

I knew the book of Micah mentions injustice. I opened my Bible to this small book and found familiar verses: "Should you not know justice, you who hate good and love evil; who tear the skin from my people and the flesh from their bones?" (Micah 3:1, 2).

Chapter five of Micah foretells Christ's birth in Bethlehem hundreds of years before Mary and Joseph traveled there on that holy night. So Micah did belong in a Christmas pageant! And Pat could indeed play Micah. While crying out for justice, he pointed others to Christ as their Savior. Pat was a living example of the message all Christians should celebrate at Christmas: Immanuel—God with us (Matthew 1:23).

Yet what was I doing? Not celebrating.

Our family's annual Christmas tradition included spending part of the holiday with Pat's extended family and then with my sister and her family. They all wanted the kids and me to join them this Christmas, but I couldn't. Our large family gathering would only accentuate the void of not having Pat with us.

I wouldn't—couldn't—trim the tree or decorate in my usual Santa-wonderland fashion. I couldn't shop for gifts or even listen to Christmas carols.

The absence of holiday cheer at our house didn't go unnoticed. Our next-door neighbors, Wayne and Clare, came to the rescue. Since they checked on Ellie Mae each Sunday while I visited Pat, they took it upon themselves to "deck the halls" with Christmas surprises.

Throughout December, each time I returned home from Bastrop I found an unexpected treat. The first week, homemade Christmas cookies waited on the kitchen counter. The next, a small, fresh Christmas tree trimmed in red ribbons adorned the kitchen table. The *pièce de résistance* appeared five days before Christmas: a six-foot Santa balloon. This last surprise made me smile every time I entered the living room.

Though I avoided decorating for Christmas, I wanted to deck the fireplace with all things Texas A&M as a tribute to Andrew's upcoming graduation. It took emotional effort, however, for me to set this up without Pat. How I wished he could be with me on this day that should have been a joyous occasion for us, one of anticipating our son's final arrival home from College Station.

One week before Christmas, Andrew pulled into the driveway in his filled-to-capacity truck. He was pleased to see the fireplace display, knowing it was hard for me, physically and otherwise. The tributes included a poem from Pat to commemorate Andrew's accomplishments. His father's thoughtful lines provided the highlight of Andrew's simple graduation "celebration."

When Andrew and I sat down to eat the dinner I had prepared, we were content, relieved that he was finished with school and back home to stay. Instead of grieving over the graduation ceremony he would miss the next day, we focused on the days ahead, thankful he had a job and a few weeks to wind down before starting work.

After dinner, we went outside to tackle the job of unloading his truck. Our long day was nearly done, and then we could relax—we thought.

By eleven o'clock we were both exhausted. Even so, Andrew came into my room to say goodnight and pray with me as he'd done each night, mostly by phone, since Pat left in July. We gave thanks for the blessings of that special day.

Fifteen minutes later I was dropping off to sleep when Andrew entered my room again.

"Mom . . . " His voice quivered. "There's a problem with my graduation. My online account shows that I didn't meet the requirements."

"Andrew!" I sat up straight. "How could that be true?"

"It shows an 'F' for my online English class."

"How?" I jumped out of my bed. "You made a 95 and a 92 on your first two papers."

"It shows a zero for the one I turned in at Thanksgiving!"

"But I was there. I saw you press the 'send' button!"

How could this have happened? In those moments, our few hours of peace shattered into disbelief and agony.

Though Andrew had turned in his last English paper four weeks earlier, the professor had not posted final grades before Andrew left school. She had only e-mailed the graduating seniors that week to let them know she was still grading papers.

We stayed awake most of the night, crying and listening to pouring rain. I also spent those anxious hours praying for mercy, desperate for God to deliver us from this out-of-the-dark dagger. Andrew, frantic to reverse his circumstances, wrote the professor about his grade and re-sent her the English paper. He even attached a snapshot of his computer e-mail history to prove he'd sent the paper back in November.

After finally going to bed at four in the morning, I woke up two hours later. Within minutes, I received a text from Clare saying she noticed an open door on Andrew's truck. She didn't need to tell me about the rain.

I went outside and pulled the heavy, wet floor mats from the truck before shutting the door.

Back inside, I checked on Andrew and saw him curled up asleep, still in his same clothes from the day before. I gently closed his bedroom door, not wanting to awaken him to his pain.

At nine-thirty, Andrew found me in the kitchen.

"Mom, I just heard back from my professor. She's going to accept my paper." Andrew slumped down into a chair and laid his head on the breakfast table.

Though drained and shaken, we thanked God for His deliverance. Andrew would graduate! We also thanked God for the timing. If Andrew had made that awful discovery earlier in the evening, before Pat's regular call, we might have unnecessarily burdened Pat with the bad news. Now, on this day when Andrew should have been joining his fellow graduates, immense relief displaced our sadness. We were spared further anguish.

Alan and Alix arrived the next day to spend part of Christmas week with Andrew and me. I planned a group shopping outing for us—a completely different kind of holiday get-together. I had bought gift cards, and we drew names to shop for each other before meeting for dinner.

After Alan finished his shopping, he noticed his sunglasses missing from his car, which made him recall how his dog had barked the night before at home in Austin. Then he realized his briefcase and laptop also were missing! Someone had broken into his car.

We tried to keep this latest episode from putting a damper on our evening. After dinner, we called the police to report the theft. But I had to wonder: *what's next?*

The following evening went better—dagger free. Wayne and Clare invited us over for dinner. While Wayne prepared mouthwatering crab cakes, Clare had set the table with delicate linens, fine china, and crystal. My family appreciated this visit in our neighbor's home and enjoyed sharing stories around their fireplace.

In addition to their hospitality, Wayne and Clare blessed each of us with a thoughtful gift. As we walked back to our house afterward, Andrew said the words all of us were thinking: "That felt like a normal holiday evening."

On Christmas Eve, Alan and Alix returned to Austin knowing that Andrew and I would join friends who'd invited us to their church service and dinner afterward.

Early Christmas morning, Andrew and I made the trip to be with Pat. At the Bastrop camp, instead of a warm hearth and filled stockings, we sat beneath plywood candy canes that served as holiday "cheer." I couldn't help crying during most of our visit. I hurt for our family and the other families around us. This was all so sad and so wrong.

At least Pat shared some positive news. After his worries about poor attendance for the Christmas pageant, the turnout had been good. With some sarcasm he explained, "The Christmas cookies we offered probably brought more men than expected." But the pageant had been a blessing for all who attended—finally, something so right!

The words of the prophet Pat had portrayed stayed with us as a comforting reminder of our Savior: "And he will be their peace" (Micah 5:5).

After a tearful goodbye to Pat, Andrew and I drove to

Austin to join Alan and Alix for Christmas dinner at her parents' home. Connie and Dan welcomed Andrew and me as part of their family. While we relaxed and even laughed that evening, I realized the daggers of the past week had only threatened to steal our joy. All had failed.

That very different Christmas ended with the assurance of Immanuel—God with us. We could sincerely worship and adore Him despite strange and painful circumstances. The awareness of His presence gave us hope. We could expect His faithfulness in the New Year, whatever it might bring.

# Chapter 13

# Choosing to See God's Hand

*By day the Lord directs his love, at night his song is with me—a prayer to the God of my life.*

PSALM 42:8

The long year ended, and we looked ahead with hopes of a better one. The New Year delivered at least one promise of good things to come: Andrew began his work career. How we all thanked God for his job in San Antonio! January also brought the expectation of a response to the appeal by the end of the month.

Having Andrew at home each night provided me with structure and purpose; life seemed somewhat normal. For one thing, I regained some motivation to prepare meals, which I hadn't done regularly for myself. Ellie Mae appeared happier too, eagerly greeting Andrew when he arrived home at the end of a day.

I tried not to be overly anxious about the appeal or fearful of the opposition, which I viewed as a force of evil against us. I came across helpful words from Michael Wells:

> In our hearts, God's light must arise each day, and all darkness, including fear, will disappear. . . . Just as light is inexpressibly greater than darkness, God's power is infinitely greater than the enemy's. . . . We need awareness of the enemy's activity, but more importantly we need a heart knowledge of the true omnipotence of our God.[1]

I needed to see God's light each day, especially during our colder-than-usual winter that offered too little sunshine.

Our visits at the Bastrop camp became more difficult as the temperatures fell. Inmates and their families crowded into one small room that consisted of hard plastic chairs and too few tables. We all struggled to converse among the confusion of so many voices and the clanking sounds of vending machines in constant use. My family commiserated with the crying babies and whining young children, who—bored and restless— roamed the room. Everyone seemed to feel the strain of these noisy, uncomfortable visits.

Toward the end of January, I was determined to visit Pat outdoors. I dressed in several layers, along with my coat, gloves, knit cap, and fur-lined boots. Pat wore his camp-issued long-sleeved green cotton shirt under a gray sweatshirt.

On that visit, Pat and I sat at one of the picnic tables and tried to think of positive topics of conversation as we braved the frigid wind. I asked if he had seen any cardinals since the one we saw at this same spot back in August. No, he hadn't, he said, even though he'd spent several hours outside each day through the fall and into winter.

As we talked, a male cardinal flew toward us and perched on a nearby tree limb! The redbird seemed to set his eyes on us and purposely stay long enough to be sure that we saw him. His beautiful form and color mesmerized us, and the timing of his appearance left us speechless.

We claimed the cardinal's visit—which we would have missed by staying indoors—as a reminder that God was with us. We thanked Him for that sweet interlude in the midst of the harsh reality of our situation.

Driving home later, still thinking of the latest cardinal, I recalled some lines I'd read recently about such incidents. In *Miracle Walk*, the author says, "Someone has suggested that 'coincidence is something that happens when God chooses to remain anonymous'—the miraculous in disguise. But it is only disguised to those who choose not to see God's hand at work beyond the laws of probability."[2]

As I continued driving, I wondered how the two cardinal visits at the camp could possibly be coincidental; both had appeared after Pat spoke of longing to see one. When a car maneuvered in front of me on the interstate, I couldn't help but notice the large handwritten words across its entire back window: "JESUS LOVES YOU." This provided one more reason to reject the possibility of coincidence. I chose instead "to see God's hand at work beyond the laws of probability."

I followed that car all the way back to San Antonio.

Dee Dee e-mailed our prayer warriors with a daily focus for February. She knew this month would be especially difficult for us as we continued to wait on the appeal while facing the approaching one-year mark of Pat's sentencing. Their prayer covering buffered me during the disconcerting anticipation of this date.

The bitter anniversary at least fell on a Saturday, which I planned to spend with Pat. On the drive to Bastrop, I armed myself "against the devil's schemes" (Ephesians 6:11) by listening to praise music all the way. I even sang along as I drove, something I had not done in a long time. My previous months of "sackcloth and ashes" featured little singing.

I was still singing when a large object flew off the bed of an overloaded pickup truck ahead of me. The industrial-size wheelbarrow catapulted straight toward my windshield. I could only brace myself for a collision, but in that momentary reaction I felt God speak to me: "I've got this." The wheelbarrow somehow missed my windshield and barely caught the left front bumper of my car.

My spirit exulted. "Yes, God. You've got this! And You've got our situation in Your hands as well."

Though I felt at peace, my body was shaking when I arrived at Buc-ee's in Bastrop a few minutes later. I always stopped at this gas station for something to eat and drink before arriving at the camp—and I took advantage of their clean restrooms. As I headed into the store, I was surprised to see three of Pat's close friends coming toward me. What a relief after my scare! The men had stopped in after their morning visit with Pat. They proceeded to check out my car from front to back. As I watched them, I anticipated telling Pat about God's presence with me on the road and His provision for me now—signs of His goodness on this dreaded anniversary.

Between averting disaster on the highway and Nancy's positive updates on the appeal, I felt things were looking up for us. My revived spirit affected everything I did.

The following week I determined to prepare better meals for Andrew. One evening I used a gloved mitt to remove baked pasta from the oven. However, a minute later, I grabbed the hot skillet handle with my bare hand. The resulting burns grew more painful with each passing hour.

At least the meal tasted delicious and provided leftovers for a few days while I was off duty from the kitchen. But a burned hand also meant that other healthy activities like piano and yoga—things that helped me relax—were out for now.

Though it seemed like I couldn't make it through one day without some new dagger thrown at me, I grew to trust that God had all of this too. I remained safe in His more than capable hands.

Besides dangerous obstacles on the highway and at home, I needed God to shield me from painful dates on the calendar. Each new month seemed to bring at least one more cause for sadness. In March, I grieved that Pat would spend his birthday in prison.

On the morning of Pat's birthday, March 18, a friend sent me a text asking me to read and pray through Psalm 18 for Pat, as she had done. However, she hadn't realized that our battle cry came from Psalm 18:2: "The Lord is my rock, my fortress and my deliverer; my God is my rock, in whom I take refuge." This fresh reminder of God's Word gave me sustenance for the day.

Pat's birthday falls during Lent, which recalls the suffering of Christ—His mock trial and hasty crucifixion. This season held new meaning for us in our suffering. Pat had tasted some of Christ's afflictions: betrayals, threats, intimidations, false accusations, an unfair sentencing, and punishment for a crime he did not commit. We prayed constantly that God would be glorified through our pain, that His saving grace would be evident to all.

In the acclaimed book *Desiring God,* John Piper shares insights on suffering: "God intends for the afflictions of Christ to be presented to the world through the afflictions of His people. . . . Our calling is to make the afflictions of Christ real for people by the afflictions we experience in bringing them the message of salvation."[3]

One morning during Lent I woke up singing the words, "By his wounds we are healed." Ten minutes later, in my prayer chair and ready for my daily infusion of strength, I opened to my reading for the day. The passage just happened to include Isaiah 53:5: "But he was pierced for our transgressions, he was crushed for our iniquities; the punishment that brought us peace was upon him, and by his wounds we are healed."

Jesus fulfilled the words spoken through the prophet Isaiah. Through His death and resurrection, we are healed and have the promise of eternal life in Him. I believed He would also heal my wounds.

Thursday of Holy Week commemorates the Passover meal, the Last Supper, that Jesus shared with his disciples in the upper room on the evening of his arrest. A devotional reading by Elizabeth Sherrill says this day, often called Maundy Thursday, marked a turning point for the disciples, who thought they could face anything until that time. She wrote:

> Thursday is the most perilous day of our pilgrimage. Because, when the test comes, we so often fail. . . . Yet

strangely, Thursday also ushers in the most hopeful stage of our journey. . . . We have learned better than to place our trust in ourselves.[4]

The word Maundy means "command." Jesus commands us to remember Him with communion, which many denominations do on Holy Thursday. One of our former pastors said the Easter celebration on Sunday morning is more meaningful if we recall Christ's suffering during Holy Week services, specifically Maundy Thursday.

Since our church met in a public school auditorium each Sunday, we could not host a Thursday service. However, I yearned to be in a house of God at this time, and I asked Dee Dee to join me at a local church that offered a Maundy Thursday service. The noon observance we attended brought a holy pause to both of us.

With my soul refreshed, I arrived home energized for the creative project I had planned. I spent the entire evening in the kitchen making three Easter basket cakes decorated with candy eggs, ribbons, and twisted wire handles. I anticipated the pleasure of presenting them to friends. These creative activities always give me joy. For that one evening, the former Luann was back.

Pat also had a blessed Maundy Thursday. Whether by coincidence or not, he gave his testimony to the men at Bible study that day, which was not the usual day to meet. His scheduled time to speak had been delayed for several weeks due to room renovations. After their meeting, several inmates told Pat they couldn't see why he was in prison—unless God had put him there to remind them of His presence.

Also during that Holy Week, Patti shared her thoughts with me about the significance of tambourines. She'd lately come across several references in her Bible reading.

"I think your welcome home party for Pat should include tambourines," she said.

Now I had to admit something. "I ordered thirty-six 'party favor' tambourines a month ago! I didn't tell anyone because I felt foolish for thinking we'd be celebrating. I put them away in a hall closet."

This news amazed Patti. The next morning she called back with more excitement in her voice. She wanted to share another significant Scripture she came upon in her English Standard Version—without searching for it. Isaiah 30:32 says: "And every stroke of the appointed staff that the Lord lays on them will be to the sound of tambourines and lyres. Battling with brandished arm, he will fight with them."

The verse referred to a victory over the enemy. But Patti couldn't wait to give me the explanation from her Bible's commentary: God Himself will fight the enemy. The role of His people is simply to celebrate!

God's Word continued to bolster me. And the idea of a celebration gave me something brighter to think about.

Around that time, several other praying friends and family members began to share similar bold words with me: a victory is coming; wait for it. These encouragements marked the beginning of my party planning—by faith. And a two-word phrase began to write itself upon my spirit: It's coming.

Our Easter Sunday, like Christmas, was different this year. Away from home again, I spent the weekend in Austin with Alan and Alix. In the early morning, before anyone else was awake, I went to sit outside on the screened-in porch.

As I sipped my coffee, I saw a frantic bird in the corner trying to free itself from the enclosure—a female cardinal! Perched on the window frame, she flapped her wings in vain.

Then, unbelievably, a bright red male cardinal flew down next to her, but on the other side of the screen. My heart melted as I gently opened the door to reunite the pair.

Later that morning, Andrew and I joined Alan and Alix at their church to worship God as a family. Afterward, Alix's parents treated all of us to an elaborate brunch. Though I enjoyed these Easter traditions, Pat's absence created a noticeable void.

I wanted to fly to my mate!

Shortly after Easter I awoke with yet another lyric running through my mind: *"And we shall see the glory of the Lord revealed."* In my quiet time later, I reread the prayer Pat wrote the night before; it included one line that echoed my morning song: *"In this process, Lord, guide us to show your glory and to show everyone how You have steered this ship to victory."*

That same morning, I also reread a passage from *Beautiful Battle:* "The battles we engage in aren't about us; they're about the glory of God. . . . Even when we plead for God to rescue us, our heart should be bent toward His glory, not merely our rescue."[5]

Waking with a song amazed me since I so often went to bed in tears. And a sudden crop of pleasant dreams also infused me with hope. I hadn't dreamt of Pat—good or bad—since he left home. I now had four dreams about him in succession. In the first one, I saw him in our den . . . laughing! Next, I saw him in church . . . singing. Then I saw him painting a room. In the fourth dream, we helped friends remodel their home. All of these dreams reflected our normal lives.

Grateful for the songs and dreams, I prayed God would

comfort and speak to Pat too. He did. Later that week, Pat wrote a new poem.

### Redemption

*We go through life with wonder*
*On which path to partake;*
*In this we ask our Savior*
*To guide us—for His sake.*

*So, what's our destination?*
*We pray this will be seen.*
*God tells us not to worry*
*For we have been redeemed.*

*Let's drop those anxious feelings*
*That gnaw at us each night.*
*With Jesus in our corner*
*We will not lose this fight.*

All of our encouragements were like manna from Heaven; they sustained us for a few hours or a day. However, like the Israelites in the desert, we would need fresh manna the next day to keep our spirits from withering.

# Chapter 14

# Rules of Engagement

*The weapons we fight with are not the weapons
of the world. On the contrary, they have
divine power to demolish strongholds.*

2 Corinthians 10:4

After nine months of waiting for Pat to come home, I was not doing well. Though I trusted God, the prolonged stress caused a crushing fatigue that settled in on me. I cried nearly every day and found it difficult to walk from one room to another. I had no energy for grocery shopping or even simple errands. Nothing made sense in my life, and this senselessness brought a depression that saturated my soul.

A secondary pain plagued me: I worried what others thought of my condition. Too weak to mask my distress, I avoided opportunities to see or even talk to many longtime friends. I feared they might judge me by mistaking my pain and sorrow for a lack of faith.

I also battled against judging myself too harshly, and I wondered if my faith was sufficient to face prolonged adversity. Some days I felt tempted to fall away into utter detachment from caring about anything. I desired to flee to some remote place where distressing circumstances could not reach me. Reading the psalms of lament helped me go easier on myself.

Some of David's psalms recall his hardships while running from King Saul for so long. His anguish reminded me that trusting God doesn't mean you don't feel pain. I kept trusting God, and so did Pat and our family. We trusted that He would someday and somehow make all the crooked ways straight. But, like David, my soul was suffering, and I cried out with his words: "How long, O Lord, how long? . . . I am worn out from groaning; all night long I flood my bed with weeping and drench my couch with tears" (Psalm 6:3, 6).

Dutifully—out of habit—I went to my comfortable prayer chair each morning for the most important hour of my day. A devotional booklet, *Our Daily Bread*, boosted my spirit during this season. One day's reading made me realize I was enrolled in The School of Pain—minus the chalkboard! The devotion included Isaiah 48:10: "See, I have refined you, though not as silver; I have tested you in the furnace of affliction."

On the following Saturday, I listed ten blessings as one of my assignments in this "school." Recording these each week usually made me feel better, but doing so didn't help my entrenched depression this time.

Later that morning I grabbed a broom to clean up the backyard patio. Maybe I could sweep away my gloom. While I worked, I saw doves and one bird I didn't recognize. I also heard another bird's constant chirping, but I refused to look up. Instead, I complained silently. *No, God. I'm not looking up. I know it's not a cardinal; it's those other birds. And besides, I'm too sad.* But the chirping continued.

I finally looked up, and there on the rooftop sat a bright red cardinal—singing. I cried at the sight and thought of Cinderella with her broom. I had been Cinderella in a third-grade play, and I was remembering how her bird friends helped her clean house. But this bird was real! And its timely presence pulled my spirit out of a dark place.

As weeks went by without any progress on his appeal, Pat's spirit grew faint like mine. Around this time Patti purchased a powerful book, *The Red Sea Rules*, which provides a biblical blueprint of ten rules for getting through a crisis. After telling me about it, she ordered a copy for Pat.

I went to a local Christian bookstore the same day and snapped up the only two available copies. The introduction captivated me: "These aren't ten quick-and-easy steps to instant solutions. . . . The reality of the Red Sea, in a word, is this: God will always make a way for His tired, yet trusting, children, even if He must split the sea to do it."[1]

We needed a parting-of-the-sea miracle! And that little gift book soothed our frazzled nerves as we struggled through disappointing delays. Pat and I could identify with the terrified Israelites and needed to remember God's instructions to them, which, in the author's paraphrasing, says, "Get a grip on yourself. Reel in these runaway emotions. Bring yourself under control. Work your way from fear to faith. Trust Me, for I'm going to take care of this. I'm going to fight for you."[2]

*The Red Sea Rules* strengthened our resolve to trust in God. It reminded us to praise God for His deliverance by recalling what He did for the Israelites: "I will sing to the Lord, for he is highly exalted. The horse and its rider he has hurled into the sea. The Lord is my strength and my song; he has become my salvation. He is my God, and I will praise him, my father's God, and I will exalt him" (Exodus 15:1, 2).

Reading those verses reminded me of the naming exercise during the retreat. Though I might be considered "renowned in battle," the war was continuing to rage. We sensed evil nipping at our heels and sometimes biting us, though we knew God ultimately controlled our circumstances.

One more of those bites came at the end of April.

Pat had tried to help an elderly man by offering to make him some locker shelves like those of other inmates. He salvaged some square, plastic pieces he retrieved from the trash after first asking the work detail "boss" for permission. This supervisor assured Pat: Of course—no problem.

But Pat soon encountered a problem. When he walked into the main building with the shelf materials, a female guard asked what he was doing. She accused him of bringing the plastic squares in to sell and make money.

"I am writing you up and taking away your phone privileges for ninety days," she announced.

Pat couldn't believe her words. Another false accusation with an unjust punishment!

Before Pat called to let me know what happened, I had e-mailed him the words of the prophet Elijah during the prophet's time of discouragement and fatigue: "I have had enough, Lord" (1 Kings 19:4). That's exactly how I felt. Now, angry at this fresh injustice, I did not handle the news well. And I took my emotions out on Pat.

"I wish you could just watch out for yourself! Why do you have to help others all the time?"

When I later told Patti about my disappointment with Pat's

mishap, her response soothed my angst.

"Luann, Pat is a righteous man. I am so proud of him. He's a light to all the men there." She also reminded me of Jesus' words: "Blessed are those who are persecuted because of righteousness, for theirs is the kingdom of heaven" (Matthew 5:10).

Twenty minutes later, I left the house to pick up my dry cleaning and visit with Maribel. I didn't tell her about Pat's trouble and the distressing phone situation. But that didn't keep her from speaking to my troubled soul.

"Luann, I have to tell you this, because it has been in my spirit this morning. Pat is a righteous man, and I am so proud of him. He is a light to all the men there."

I couldn't believe what she was saying! She repeated the exact three phrases that Patti used. Tic. Tac. Toe!

I shared their words with Pat by e-mail, adding, "I am proud of you too. And I'm glad God reminded me of who you are through Patti's and Maribel's words."

Late that evening, our Bible study friends Mark and Lynn called to pray with me, though they knew nothing about Pat's phone privileges being revoked. God did, however, and He continued to use friends like these to encourage us at specific times of need.

Since Pat could no longer call, we e-mailed our nightly prayers. I treasured his words and printed them to share with Alan and Andrew.

Another unexpected event brought one more challenge to my daily communications with Pat.

Torrential storms hit San Antonio during that month of

May and took out the electricity several times. When I looked out a bedroom window to check the rain gauge, I discovered water coming through the ceiling! As I grabbed a trash can, I wondered: *What's next?*

I had my answer when I couldn't reach Pat by e-mail. My computer seemed to be dying a quick death, perhaps facilitated by the power outages. In a panic, I reached out to Clare, next door.

"Luann, you're in luck," she said. "My friend who builds her own computers will be in town tomorrow and staying with me. She can help you."

Clare's friend did help me, but she also confirmed that I needed a new computer.

Pat shared my technology woes with one of his "mighty men." Chris just happened to be visiting Pat that Saturday, and he responded by calling his personal technician. Within two days, I had a new computer without losing any data.

Besides causing the power outages, a roof leak, and a computer crash, the storms also made the drive to Bastrop treacherous on the Sunday of Memorial Day weekend. Andrew and I were diverted from the main highway due to high water, but each detour ended with a roadblock.

I became frantic knowing this delay would rob us of our limited hours with Pat, especially since we couldn't talk to him during the week. Finally—four hours later—we arrived at the camp.

Safe at home that evening, we heard terrible news. Not far from the roadblocks we had faced, thirteen people lost their lives—swept away by a raging river.

The same storms that delivered disaster brought much needed water to areas of drought, which included the huge, empty crater behind our lake house. Only three percent full, the lake should have taken several years to refill, according to experts. But now it began to fill dramatically after each new storm. Every morning I checked a website for updated lake levels. The lake's rise gave me hope for our circumstances. I daily asked God to refill us with his Holy Spirit, drench our parched souls, and shower us with His presence.

I decided to make my first trip to the lake since Pat left home. After seeing the beautiful sight with my own eyes, I told Patti how amazing it looked. Then she reminded me of something I'd said only weeks before: "It would take a bigger miracle to fill the lake than the one we need for Pat to come home."

While the lake level continued to rise, my emotional state remained low. Knowing I struggled to stay positive, Bonnie called to say her prayer group had interceded for me that morning. She also shared the words of 2 Samuel 23:9, 10, which someone had recited in prayer for me. The passage tells about one of King David's "three mighty men," Eleazar, who stood his ground and struck down the Philistines until the Lord brought about a great victory.

When I heard Bonnie read the name Eleazar, I immediately recalled the story I read during my prayer time that same morning, only I'd read it from 1 Chronicles 11:12-14:

Next to him was Eleazar son of Dodai the Ahohite, one of the three mighty men. He was with David at Pas Dammim when the Philistines gathered there for battle. At a place where there was a field full of barley, the troops fled from the Philistines. But they took their stand in the middle of the field. They defended it and struck the Philistines down, and the Lord brought about a great victory.

Once again, I had received repetition of a seemingly random passage of Scripture. Knowing the Bible contains more than thirty-one thousand verses, I figured this made it a .003 percent chance of happening. But the odds must have been even greater since the passage came from two different books! What did God want me to see?

A clear message emerged as I looked up those First Chronicles verses in my Bible commentary: "In any struggle, fear can keep us from taking a stand for God and from participating in God's victories. Face your fear head on. If you are grounded in God, victory will come when you hold that ground."[3]

Like David's troops, I wanted to flee from the challenge before me, but God's Word showed me what could happen if I faced the enemy as Eleazar did.

I needed courage to even face my desk calendar, which unsettled me continually. A few more weeks would bring our thirty-first wedding anniversary and mark a year that would clearly fall into the "for worse" category of marriage vows. I also grieved over two upcoming wedding showers I'd scheduled but could not bring myself to attend.

At least I could be with my friends in spirit by putting together creative floral arrangements and party favors. I filled eight pairs of cowboy boots with a variety of fresh flowers. For the favors, I spent two days making one hundred and twenty chocolate-covered pretzels, complete with personalized tags. As I worked, I desperately hoped Pat would be home soon so we could attend the late summer weddings together.

The dagger date on the calendar, July 9, made me face the fact that my husband had been gone an entire year. Only God's strength kept Pat and me from losing hope as all those weeks and months had passed. We continued to cry out to Him with the psalmist's words: "How long must I wrestle with my thoughts and every day have sorrow in my heart? How long will my enemy triumph over me?" (Psalm 13:2).

On the unsettling date of July 9, a friend sent me a text message with a prayerful verse she'd chosen "for the ninth day of the seventh month." Psalm 7:9 says: "O righteous God, who searches minds and hearts, bring to an end the violence of the wicked and make the righteous secure."

I persevered by tethering myself to God's Word. One morning in my prayer chair I read a commentary about God making himself known to the prophet Elijah in spectacular ways—in a violent wind, an earthquake, and in fire (1 Kings 19:11, 12). The writer posed a question: Would we like for God to reveal himself to us in such recognizable ways?

While pondering this thought, I gazed out the window and saw a bright red cardinal on a tree branch looking directly at me!

The surreal timing of the cardinal visits made each appearance a supernatural occasion for me. So often when I found myself sinking it seemed that God used this beautiful bird as a sign of His presence, to assure me that He sees me, that He is with us.

Pat's poems, which expressed his faith, also encouraged me. Like David, he poured out his confusion and angst in verse. This one is titled "Drink Him In."

*We pray to You, Jesus*
*In heaven above,*
*We're so very grateful*
*For the abundance of love.*

*You tell us to call You*
*In times of our need,*
*But to also be patient—*
*Don't rely on world-speed.*

*But what will be gained*
*To follow God's law?*
*From the well of salvation*
*Your water we'll draw.*

*Lord, cast out the demons*
*That prowl at our heels*
*And show the whole world*
*How Your victory feels.*

*He turns curses to blessings*
*Matters not what we think*
*His promised Word tells us*
*Come to Me and drink.*

Pat persevered by helping others. Needless to say, he found plenty of opportunities.

One day during lunch break, an inmate approached Pat and asked him to pray with a group of men because of a distressing incident. An inmate had lost the truck keys entrusted to him for a work assignment. If the keys were not found, he would be punished with solitary confinement. The distraught man believed they fell out of his pocket somewhere in a grassy area the size of three football fields!

The inmates bowed their heads as Pat prayed about the

situation. While some men had to return to their work, a few others, including Pat, received permission to search the area—a blessing since the rules strictly forbid inmates from helping one another. Within one hour, an 80-year-old inmate who could barely bend over found the keys. The men gathered together again, this time to thank God for His quick answer to their prayer.

Pat and I both claimed the promises in God's Word as we held on while waiting for resolution. We could not deny His presence with us, encouraging us each day in some way.

In mid-July we received hopeful news from Nancy regarding the strength of our appeal. She explained that another case in the courts at that time could favorably affect Pat's outcome. But this encouragement did not ease my anxious thoughts. Waiting for the court's decision felt something like sitting in an ICU waiting room—day in and day out.

One Sunday in August with Pat, I met a woman who seemed anxious to speak with me. "I've been wanting to meet you," she said. "My husband and I see you and your family praying together, and I know you are Christians. Could your husband please reach out to help my husband? We are Christians too, and we believed in God's promises, but then we were devastated."

That woman's words struck my heart like a knife. They tapped into my fear that God might not fulfill His promises on our behalf. If God should fail us, what hope would we have? By the time I reached my car on that 100-plus-degree afternoon, I was crying.

When I shared the unsettling remark with a friend that

evening, she couldn't understand why the woman's loss of hope would affect my peace. But I could not shake a feeling of dread; maybe my spirit had a foreboding sense of things going wrong.

Within forty-eight hours, Nancy called.

"Luann, the Fifth Circuit Court denied the claims in Pat's appeal. This is unbelievable."

Nancy explained to me that in the court's opinion Pat's attorneys had not effectively objected on the day of his sentencing. She lamented this outcome with bitter disappointment that in some ways equaled ours. We all knew that Pat's attorneys had tried to interject an opposing argument on the day of sentencing, but the judge would not allow them to proceed.

"I have been an appellate attorney for nearly forty years," Nancy said, "and though you never say you have a case you can't lose, Pat's case was indeed a case I couldn't lose. It was un-losable!"

Her words pelted me like a cold rain. I tried to digest this second serving of injustice, but I could barely breathe. My dumbstruck mind replayed the omen of the woman at Bastrop: "We believed in God's promises, but then we were devastated."

Our hopes also had been dashed.

Still on the phone with Nancy, my heart and mind began to race as sobering realizations washed over me in waves. We would not be able to attend the upcoming weddings. We would not be home together for the holidays. And I would not be pulling the tambourines out of the closet for Pat's homecoming celebration.

Nancy's fighting spirit, however, recalled me to the present. She had no intention of giving up and going away in defeat. "By no means is it over!" she said. "We'll demand a hearing."

No cardinal arrived on that day of mourning, but the "angel" Maribel appeared on my doorstep. Together we sat on the screened-in patio with cups of coffee. While we talked, she took the napkin I gave her and began to work with it, shaping it into a boat. Then she pulled a pen from her purse and wrote on one side, "Be Still." On the other: "God Is in Control."

After we prayed, Mirabel said, "The victory belongs to the one with the last move—like a chess game. And, Luann, you know Who has the last move." She also repeated Nancy's words: "It's not over."

Still crying and shaking, I nodded, knowing Mirabel was right.

Alone the next morning, I forced myself to my prayer chair, desperate to hear from God. I could not stop the flood of terrifying thoughts. Why would He allow the injustice to continue? What would happen to us now? How could I continue to go on paying the bills and keeping up our home?

As I picked up my devotional booklet, my eyes opened wide at the day's reading, titled, "Chess Master." Those were Maribel's words from the day before, though she had never read this book! I eagerly read through to the closing lines: "With the Grand Master, victory is assured, no matter how the board of life may look at any given moment."[4]

Oh, how I prayed for the Chess Master of the Universe to make the last move!

Patti, who I talked to every day at this point, reminded me of the apostle Paul's words that she had witnessed in my life over and again the past year: "We are hard pressed on every side, but not crushed; perplexed, but not in despair; persecuted, but not abandoned; struck down, but not destroyed" (2 Corinthians 4:8, 9).

When Nancy called that afternoon to assure me of her

renewed determination to fight for us, I walked out to the patio with the phone to my ear, trying to hold back tears. Then I noticed an unexpected visitor. A cardinal swooped down to a branch in front of me and lingered—as if to make sure I noticed.

# Chapter 15

# Treading and Trampling

*Hope deferred makes the heart sick.*
PROVERBS 13:12

Confusion settled in on me like an unwelcomed houseguest. I began to doubt everything I believed God had shown me during the past year, and most assuredly I doubted God's love for me. I questioned everything, including why I should write a book. Who would want to read my sad story?

Since the book of Habakkuk initially inspired me to write, I turned to it once again. While reading, I realized the prophet felt the same way as me. He couldn't understand why God allowed the Babylonians to conquer Judah. And he questioned God: Why did the injustice last so long? But God assured Habakkuk that evil would not win in the long run and that judgment of evil was coming. The prophet regained his trust in God and concluded his book with a prayer of victory and thanksgiving.

Evil and injustice seemed to have the upper hand in my world too. In view of our insurmountable troubles, I needed to trust God. Though nothing made sense to me, I tried to keep my eyes on God and off the difficulties. My spirit *wanted* to appropriate Habakkuk's words: "Lord, I have heard of your fame; I stand in awe of your deeds, O Lord. Renew them in our day, in our time make them known; in wrath remember mercy" (Habakkuk 3:1). But my flesh often refused to cooperate.

Randy Alcorn, in *The Goodness of God*, writes, "No evil will go forever unpunished. The wheels of justice may seem to turn slowly, but they turn surely. Scripture assures us that justice is coming: 'God will bring every deed into judgment, including every hidden thing, whether it is good or evil' (Ecclesiastes 12:14). Justice is certain, even when it isn't immediate."[1]

Though heartsick, I mustered my courage and fervently prayed for God to guide my upcoming visit with Pat. Since hearing the devastating news, we had to wait five days to see each other.

Sitting at one of the picnic tables with Pat, I opened the vial of the Garden of Gethsemane oil we used to anoint one another. It seemed symbolic to us that the oil was running low.

Besides our crushed hopes, Pat's physical suffering intensified. The air conditioning unit in the sleeping quarters of his metal building remained broken for six weeks with no repair in sight; men were forced to endure temperatures of more than a hundred degrees. On top of the heat—possibly because of it—came an outbreak of scabies, a severe, itchy rash caused by mites that burrow into the skin.

Pat and I tried to be strong for each other, but we could not stop the tears. At least we could laugh a bit, though bitterly, about the prison staff's attempt to eradicate the scabies. The inmates received orders to turn in their pillows, bedding, and clothing. When these items came back, Pat needed to wring his pillow to remove the water. It had been hosed down!

Three weeks later the camp still had no air conditioning. And—no surprise—the scabies continued.

In his same book on God's goodness, Alcorn says, "God doesn't merely empathize with our sufferings. He actually suffers. Jesus is God; what he suffered, God suffered. God paid the highest price on our behalf; we therefore have no grounds for believing he doesn't 'get it.' . . . Whenever you feel tempted in your suffering to ask God, 'Why are you doing this to me?' look at the Cross and ask, 'Why did you do that for me?'"[2]

God revealed His goodness to me through friends like Clare who offered comfort. Seeing my weakened condition after the lost appeal, she surprised me by booking a fall retreat for the two of us at a spa near Austin. I couldn't imagine enjoying three days of relaxation that included yoga and a massage while Pat languished in harsh conditions. Yet I needed relief from my crippling anxieties.

Days before the result of the appeal, Patti felt the Holy Spirit leading her to put together a different forty-day prayer focus, one based on psalms of praise. She mentioned Psalm 8:2, which says of the Lord, "You have ordained praise because of your enemies, to silence the foe and the avenger." With my agreement, she selected passages from forty psalms and e-mailed them each day to Dee Dee, who sent them to our prayer team.

Even before the devastating news, I had not been in the mood to praise God. But I knew from Scripture that praise is

a remedy for worry and fear, which still consumed me much
of the time.

Our faithful prayer warriors began to praise God for what
He would do in our behalf, though most were unaware of the
failed appeal. (Nancy had suggested we wait to share this news
until we knew the next step.)

The selected passages were powerful reminders that: God
is a shield around us (Psalm 3:3), He makes us dwell in safety
(Psalm 4:8), He is a refuge for the oppressed in times of trouble
(Psalm 9:9), and so much more. The forty days of praise provided a daily dose of encouragement that helped combat our
anguish as we dwelled on the God who is greater than every
evil circumstance.

Knowing that I desperately needed to let go of my anxieties,
I wrote these words in my journal:

*Jesus, You are my burden-bearer. I can't carry this
burden. I feel myself breaking because I don't know how
to lay it down without falling apart.*

My continual state of anxiety-induced weakness often
made me feel like a failure in all of my relationships—except as
Pat's wife. This self-absorbed condition kept me from reaching
out to others. I also felt hypocritical in my faith by not always
resting in God's assurances. How could I hope to inspire others
with my story when I kept floundering?

And then I would recall how Paul and his companions
experienced similar emotions. He wrote, "We were under great
pressure, far beyond our ability to endure, so that we despaired
even of life. Indeed, in our hearts we felt the sentence of death.
But this happened that we might not rely on ourselves but on
God, who raises the dead" (2 Corinthians 1:8, 9).

Two weeks after receiving Nancy's bad-news phone call, I was housecleaning when a four-inch-long scorpion crept across the foyer floor. I grabbed a nearby book to crush it, and, though my heart pounded, it felt good to take out some pent-up frustration on the venomous pest.

A few days later I opened a book on God's promises and gave my full attention to the first verse I came to, words of Jesus to his disciples: "I saw Satan fall like lightning from heaven. I have given you authority to trample on snakes and scorpions and to overcome all the power of the enemy; nothing will harm you" (Luke 10:18).

I had trampled a scorpion—with a book! All I needed now was a snake to go with it, which the Lord would soon provide, perhaps to emphasize the truth of His Word.

Clare, always trying to lift my spirit, encouraged me to take walks with her. When the weather permitted, we walked several miles on Saturdays. The fresh air and exercise strengthened me physically and improved my perspective, and my fifteen-pound Ellie Mae benefitted from the outings too.

On one walk, Clare and I discussed the warning sign posted at the entrance of our neighborhood: "Watch out for mountain lions!" In eighteen years of living here, I had never heard of mountain lions in the area. So we kept a sharp eye as we walked, which proved beneficial.

"Luann!" Clare shouted and yanked my arm to pull me away from the curb and into the street. "There's a coral snake in front of you!"

The snake, about four feet long, slinked away into the grass, but I couldn't stop shaking. I'd never seen one of those "red-on-yellow-kill-a-fellow" snakes in South Texas.

The next day Clare mentioned she researched coral snakes and found they belonged to the cobra family. Later in the same day, I heard from Dee Dee, who, unaware of the analogies I'd seen, sent a psalm of encouragement: "You will tread upon the lion and the cobra; you will trample the great lion and the serpent" (Psalm 91:13). Here was that word "trample" again!

I prayed that God intended those run-ins with creatures as object lessons to assure me of His protection despite the threats we faced, and that we would indeed trample evil. But a more frightful encounter—and a greater display of God's presence—was coming soon.

Alan and Alix arrived to stay with us the day before their friend's wedding in San Antonio. Knowing Alix wanted a pedicure before the event, I picked a nearby salon I'd never visited. Though I would not be attending the wedding, I made appointments for both of us and then had to reschedule for an earlier time so Alix would not be rushed. I intended this to be a special time with my daughter-in-law, but it proved to be divine in another way.

At the salon, I selected nail polish from a shelf before proceeding toward my pedicure chair. I couldn't help but notice the only man in the salon, who sat with his feet wrapped in hot towels. I knew this man too well! My heart began to race, and my legs trembled beneath me at my proximity to the federal prosecutor whose actions had harmed my family.

I sat down by Alix, who, after finding out what troubled me, comforted me with a calm voice. Within fifteen minutes, the prosecutor left the salon—without noticing me.

In the pedicure chair, I took deep breaths in an attempt to calm myself. How could I have run into that man a second time and in such an unlikely place?

Once again, God's Word would soon supply an answer.

My unscheduled reading the next morning from Psalm 23 confirmed the "coincidence" at the salon was not a chance encounter. Verse five of this familiar passage reinforced God's personal assurance to me: "You prepare a table before me in the presence of my enemies."

I'd read that same Scripture in a different book the morning after seeing the prosecutor in the restaurant on the day the appeal was originally filed—exactly one year ago.

Now we awaited another filing within days. We had recently agreed with Nancy's next step: to request a rehearing of Pat's appeal. Adding to this strange timing, the filing would once again occur at the onset of Yom Kippur, the Jewish Day of Atonement.

These incredible run-ins with the prosecutor made me search for stories about David, who wrote Psalm 23. Before becoming King of Israel, David encountered his enemy, King Saul, who jealously pursued him to take his life. God allowed David the opportunity to come upon the king by surprise—not once, but twice (1 Samuel 24:4; 26:7). Each time, David could have confronted Saul or attacked him, but he chose to trust God to avenge the wrongs.

Was God testing me to see how I would respond in the presence of my enemy? Was he showing me that He would judge the wrong done to Pat?

I couldn't wait to see Pat the next day to share the details of

Saturday's incident and the repetition of Psalm 23. Since our evening phone calls were both limited and monitored, he had saved a story for me too.

At our picnic table on Sunday, I munched vending machine popcorn as Pat shared the climax of his week: an inmate collapsed outdoors while watching a few others play basketball. Pat had raced to the guard's office to request the defibrillator as two doctors—also inmates—began to administer CPR. The unconcerned guard told him not to worry, that he had called the paramedics. When Pat insisted on taking the defibrillator and the guard did not offer it, he grabbed the device from the wall, risking certain punishment. He ran about a hundred yards back to the stricken man, hoping it wasn't too late. With the defibrillator, the doctors resuscitated the man.

After Pat finished telling that story, he noticed both doctors' wives were also visiting, and he wanted to tell the women they should be proud of their husbands. As I watched him go over to one of the couple's table, the doctor motioned for me to join them as well.

"Pat was the real hero that day," the man told me. He said they could not have saved the man if Pat hadn't retrieved the defibrillator so quickly.

We were thankful the guards did not punish Pat. Instead, they later apologized to him for not acting with more urgency.

But Pat's story wasn't over. He had been scheduled to give the message at the weekly chapel service the day after that medical emergency. Instead of the typical sparse attendance, the designated room was filled to capacity!

# Chapter 16

# Words for the Weary

*Trust in him at all times, O people; pour out*
*your hearts to him, for God is our refuge.*
PSALM 62:8

During that time of waiting and hoping for good news regarding the rehearing of our appeal, I did not sleep well. The worries that tried to consume my peace by day also attempted to steal my rest at night, when I had little resistance to repel them. If I sought to extinguish one worry, another would flare up. Besides my fears about the legal outcome, I worried about finances and how to get through the approaching holidays. Worst of all—and hard to admit—I worried that God's promises might not come through for us. After all, there had been ample opportunities for Him to bring about justice.

This continual drain on my faith featured too much crying, which exhausted my body and wearied my soul. Often when I woke up in tears during the night, I made myself sing the simple but reassuring children's verse: *Jesus loves me this I know; for the Bible tells me so. Little ones to Him belong. They are weak but He is strong. Yes, Jesus loves me. Yes, Jesus loves me. Yes, Jesus loves me, the Bible tells me so.*

Besides reminding myself that Jesus loved me, it also helped to remember that heroes of the Bible had similar struggles. David wrote, "Evening, morning and noon I cry out in distress and he hears my voice" (Psalm 55:17).

Randy Alcorn writes, "Worry is momentary atheism crying out for correction by trust in a good and sovereign God."[1]

My doubts about God were often momentary—but sometimes lasted for days. I wondered if He needed an update on our dire situation: the Egyptian army is closing in on us and we are facing the Red Sea! I tried to reassure myself that God could have reasons to delay our deliverance. And I pondered how God led the Israelites on a circuitous route to the Promised Land because it was safer for them.

One night I did sleep, and I had an unusual dream. This dream had no people, no circumstances, no action, and no dilemma. Instead, I saw only two clear words, one over the other, like a billboard: TRUST ME.

Not knowing how or what to pray on the morning after seeing those vivid words, I asked God to help me trust Him in all things. I meditated on Nahum 1:7: "The Lord is good, a refuge in times of trouble. He cares for those who trust in him."

I wrote the words TRUST ME in capital letters in my journal every day for two weeks, hoping that if I wrote them I would believe them and indeed trust God. If waves of panic hit me during the day, or if fear overwhelmed me during the night, I remembered my TRUST ME dream.

Several days later, a friend, unaware of my dream, sent a text that referred to several promises of God: "Just trust Me, be still and know that I am for you and with you always."

In mid-November, within a month of that encouraging dream, I received a late-night text from Bonnie's daughter, Brooke, who sensed that God had spoken to her during her prayer time. Her brief message: "Jesus said to tell you that He knows—tell her I'm here."

I thanked Brooke for being bold in her faith, but I wondered why the Holy Spirit prompted her at 9:30 on a Thursday night!

When Pat called the next day, I knew why Brooke's message had been so urgent.

"Luann, the Fifth Circuit Court panel denied reviewing the decision on our appeal."

"Pat . . . did they say why?"

"They only said the same thing, that our attorneys should have objected. I'm sick to my stomach and can't think of what is going on in this world of injustice."

"Oh, Pat. I'm confused too. But I have to tell you that Brooke sent me a text late last night telling me Jesus says He is here, and He knows." These few words now provided a measure of comfort to us by showing us one more sign of God's presence.

Though we had known that less than two percent of requests to review an appeal are accepted, we hoped to be in that percentage. Once again, our hopes were dashed.

Hours later on that same November day, news broke of widespread terrorism in Paris that took more than a hundred lives and injured hundreds more. This deadliest attack on France since World War II added to a pervasive sense of gloom in the world that paralleled our own bleak outlook. The forces of evil seemed to be prevailing.

My routine of twenty-plus years carried me forward the next day. I rose before dawn and made coffee without asking myself how I felt. I put one foot in front of the other in the direction of my prayer chair. Like those who run marathons, I was "hitting the wall," but I knew my habit of morning devotion would help me push through.

I picked up my pen to write the words Brooke had given me: "Tell her I'm here, and He knows." Then I added the words TRUST ME. I prayed for God to keep us hopeful and for his help in keeping me from the anger and depression that could easily grow in such bitter circumstances. Casting off these negative emotions was not easy.

With Thanksgiving a week away, I naturally desired to be with my family. At the same time, I did not want to risk repeating the confusion and sadness of the previous year. Andrew and I had been invited by Alan and Alix to join her family in Austin, but I feared my current struggle against despair would dampen their holiday.

Instead, since Andrew accepted another invitation, I joined Wayne and Clare for a quiet dinner in their home. As I crossed the street with an appetizer and dessert I'd prepared for our small Thanksgiving feast, I somehow managed to leave the bitterness behind at my house.

For two hours I felt blessed and pampered to enjoy Cornish hens and all the holiday trimmings on a table of fine china and crystal. I was so thankful to be adopted for the day by such kind friends.

Over dinner, I shared my TRUST ME dream with Clare and confessed to her that, although I had made a conscious choice to trust God, I now struggled to keep trusting Him. Clare gave me simple, Holy Spirit-inspired advice: "Choose again."

I took Clare's words home with me and later added them to the growing faith repertoire in my journal: "TRUST ME"; "Tell her I'm here"; "He knows"; "Choose again."

In my former life, the Christmas season commenced on the Friday after Thanksgiving. But I could no longer conjure up the joy that holidays require. Besides our ongoing legal issues, we had an unsettling new dilemma.

Nancy now recommended an appeal to the United States Supreme Court, explaining how our case merited consideration. This sounded so unreal I could barely speak of it to friends and family members.

So, while the world around me began to shop, decorate, and bake Christmas cookies, I needed to focus on the particulars of a higher appeal process.

Kenny drove from Austin to join me for a meeting with Nancy, who had recently moved her office into an old home in one of San Antonio's historic districts. Despite boxes and equipment stacked haphazardly around us, we all sat down to discuss a Supreme Court appeal.

Nancy remained beaten down from the second defeat of the appeal that should have easily exposed the injustice against Pat. She offered no assurance of success this time, but said, "We have a glimmer of hope, Luann."

I didn't like the word *glimmer*; it sounded weak. But days later I read these words in my Bible's introduction to the book of Zephaniah: "Overwhelming grief, prolonged distress, incessant abuse, continual persecution, and imminent punishment breed hopelessness and despair. . . . With just a glimmer of hope, we would take courage and carry on, enduring until the end."[2]

Three weeks before Christmas we finalized the decision to file a petition with the Supreme Court. Now I could try to find the Christmas spirit. I thought of the poems Pat had written in the past year and decided to have them printed as gift books for our boys, Pat's mother and brothers, and my sister. This would be my only gift to each of them, but it would also be from Pat.

I hurried to arrange, type, and choose artwork for each page. Even so, I nearly ran out of time to complete the book project and order copies, which were scheduled for delivery on Christmas Eve.

Alan and Alix surprised me one afternoon a few days before Christmas by arriving earlier than expected. Their car was filled to the brim with packages and a holiday tree complete with lights!

Alan smiled and gave me a hug before explaining, "Mom, you and Andrew didn't put up a tree last year, and there were no packages. We aren't going to do that again! We came early to decorate the tree before Andrew gets home. We'll put all of the family ornaments on the tree, and you can help unless it makes you too sad."

With happy tears, I helped unload more packages than I could count. While I had tried so hard to find joy, it came and found me.

After an early breakfast on Christmas morning, the four of us made the two-hour drive to Bastrop. Our gratitude to be together as a family helped ease the pain of seeing Pat in this prison camp for another Christmas. And we all had that "glimmer of hope" as we faced the new year. But our holiday gathering wasn't without one of those arrows that flies by day.

I had purchased copies of *Jesus Calling* as gifts for two inmates' wives who I knew struggled with their faith in their adverse circumstances. I wrapped the devotional books in brown paper, printed Pat's Christmas poem as a decoration on top of each, and then placed each book in a clear plastic zip bag in case of rain. Before leaving the house that day, I sent a text message for my new friends to look for their gifts in the parking lot by the right front tire of my car since rules forbade bringing gifts into the facility

Outside in the cold weather, bundled in coats and scarves, my family was sitting at a picnic table enjoying our visit when three guards approached. One of the men addressed me in a stern voice.

"Mrs. Mire, I need for you to come speak with me. And bring one of your sons with you."

I stood up, trembling, and walked with Andrew toward the guards.

"Did you bring these?" The guard pointed to the books— now unwrapped.

Not knowing I had done anything wrong, I began to cry and tried to defend myself.

"These are Christmas gifts for two women who are hurting so much, and they need these devotional books about God's love for them."

The guards agreed to allow the wives to keep the books minus the wrapping and Pat's poem.

Before we left that day, one of the guards apologized to me for the way they handled the situation. I thanked him for his words, and, knowing the wrapping paper was in the guards' office, I asked him to please read Pat's poem.

I later realized the irony of receiving a reprimand for trying to share Jesus on the very day the world celebrates His birth.

That little taste of persecution made me think of missionaries who risk persecution for taking Bibles and faith-related materials into countries that restrict religious freedom. While I could have lost my visiting privileges, many believers suffer severe consequences for sharing their faith.

In another ironic twist regarding my scare with the guards, Pat found favor with several inmates who had never before spoken to him. After I left that day, the men approached him to say they couldn't believe how I had been treated. They mentioned always noticing a smile on my face and seeing how I tried to encourage others. Pat and I appreciated their support, but we also realized our faith was evident to others who were watching.

I was so thankful Pat did not lose privileges because of my deed. And I wondered if my botched attempt to bless two women may have served as a Christmas gift for the guards. I prayed for them to see light in that dark place by reading Pat's poem.

### The True Light

*I look at the calendar and can't believe my eyes.*
*It's that time of year when we look to the skies.*
*Whether cold or warm, December is here,*
*And we file into churches to draw Him near.*

*He's here the year 'round, even when we feel apart.*
*The Holy Spirit indwells us when He enters our heart.*
*We don't need a miracle to know He's Supreme.*
*We can just close our eyes and with faith He is seen.*

*So, look to the skies to see what's so bright:*
*The shining star of Jesus reveals God's true Light.*

# Chapter 17

# Hope for Frodo

*He is before all things, and in him*
*all things hold together.*

Colossians 1:17

Fresh hope came in mid-January with the filing of Pat's petition to the Supreme Court. This formidable next step in our fight for justice was beyond my comprehension. Nancy explained that clerks in this highest court screen all petitions and decide which ones to send to the nine justices.

The New Year included some new anxieties as I anticipated the challenge of returning to work. A family friend had offered me a part-time role with his company, and, aware of my fragile state, he would allow some work-schedule flexibility. Ready or not, I needed to accept this kind offer as God's provision.

January also delivered some timely encouragement. I'd received a new daily devotional study of the Psalms as a Christmas gift from Bonnie. *The Songs of Jesus,* by Tim Keller, proved to be the perfect companion to help me face each day.

As my first week of work approached, I felt waves of panic. I had lost my confidence and worried whether I'd be able to interact with coworkers in a professional way without making a spectacle of myself by crying. And how would I even be able to concentrate on learning new tasks?

One morning's reading in *The Songs of Jesus* seemed written just for me: "But I won't panic—or should I say, 'Lord help me not to panic.' I know You are on your throne, but my heart doesn't feel that—so speak to my heart. Let me love you enough not to be scared."[1]

It seemed beyond coincidence when Patti received the same devotional as a Christmas gift from a friend. Since I called her for prayer and encouragement nearly every day now—sometimes more than once—we realized this through-the-year study would allow us to share insights and pray together according to the psalms.

Patti knew my struggle so well that she would often underline the same words or passages in *The Songs of Jesus* that I had marked during my reading. For example, we both highlighted these lines: "Believing the promise of your presence in my suffering takes time and grows slowly through stages in prayer. So I will pray until my heart rejoices in you."[2] Time and again, Patti and I realized that having a sense of God's presence was all that kept me from drowning in my circumstances.

Wanting to start the year off right, I reflected on Clare's gentle admonition: "Choose again." Her words had spoken to me on more than one level. Besides choosing daily to trust God, I needed to keep choosing to forgive others.

I knew well the words of Jesus: "But I tell you: Love your enemies and pray for those who persecute you, that you may be sons of your Father in heaven" (Matthew 5:44, 45). I had to forgive and love those who had wronged us, to see them through Christ-filtered lenses. Yet I still found myself dealing with the same unforgiveness toward the same people, and this threatened to turn me into a bitter person. I had to choose again and again to forgive.

The week before I began work, my friend Tricia—totally unaware of my job—called me with a wonderful offer.

"Luann, I have been praying for you, and I believe God put it on my heart to start bringing you and Andrew dinner every Monday night. Would that be OK?"

"Oh, Tricia, you have no idea how much that would help," I said. "I'm starting a new job next week."

Tricia had no way of knowing how perfectly timed her gesture would be, including the day of the week. Since I spent every Sunday at Bastrop, I always felt drained the next day, which I'd begun referring to as "meltdown Monday." I had already expected that working on Mondays would be a major challenge. Tricia's gracious offer showed me that God was more than aware of my needs.

On my first day of work, I found myself alone on the elevator to the ninth floor of the stately office building. This allowed me to give myself some last-minute instructions—out loud— before the doors opened. "Stand up straight, Luann, put a smile on your face, greet others, and walk with your head held high." The things I used to do without thinking now required conscious effort.

At the end of my first workday, Tricia met me at my house with her home-cooked meal: stuffed pork tenderloin, roasted vegetables, spinach salad, and fresh rolls. Her sacrificial giving became a weekly ritual of exchanging clean, empty dishes for those filled with delicious food. This act of kindness earned a regular spot in the weekly blessing column of my prayer journal.

Despite the encouragements, I felt overwhelmed by the end of my first week of work. On Saturday I woke up too early and in an anxious state; even morning devotion time did not calm my spirit. I picked up my phone to unleash my emotions in a text to Patti.

At some point, Patti had begun referring to me as "Frodo" and herself as "Sam"; these, of course, are the two main characters in *The Lord of the Rings* trilogy. She explained that, like Sam, she could only keep me company and encourage me as I journeyed on; she could not take my burden. The humorous names helped me view myself as someone in an epic adventure. However, like Frodo, I was not sure about surviving my role.

My long text to Patti that morning was all Frodo.

*I don't understand our loving God. How can I begin to tell others of His love and presence when I hurt this much? I have no hope. I'm avoiding people .... I thought our story would be about redemption and restoration through God's intervention, but all I see is the power of evil—how it kills, steals and destroys. I can't keep pretending that God will rescue us. That's just in Disney movies. I have looked to God to save us but I'm not being saved. This disappointment feels foolish. I should not have gotten my hopes up. I want to shout "God wins!" But that is not the world I'm in. Sadly, I envy Pat. No pressures of home around him. Three meals a day. Friends in the same situation. Bible studies. I'm just a worn-out, grieving person who can barely make it to work and back. Is there a place where Frodos can go to heal?*

Whenever I doubted God, I descended into a pit of despair. Once my thinking improved—usually after a more restful day or a good night of sleep—I would realize my doubts were not uncommon.

On that fretful day, I doubted that our story could ever help anyone else, even though I had felt God's direction to write a book and His encouragement all along as I worked on it. Regarding this task, I saw a picture of myself in Moses, who complained to God about his assignment.

Moses argued with God: "Who am I, that I should go to Pharaoh and bring the Israelites out of Egypt?" (Exodus 3:11); "What if they do not believe me or listen to me and say, 'The Lord did not appear to you'" (Exodus 4:1).

But the Lord didn't accept Moses' excuses. Instead, He brought Moses' brother, Aaron, to help. So Moses obeyed God—but then had a meltdown after Pharaoh's response made things worse instead of better for the Israelites.

Moses expressed his disappointment and anger to God: "You have not rescued your people at all" (Exodus 5:23).

I understood how Moses felt. Who was I to think I was qualified to write a book? And if I did, what if no one would believe my words about the injustices and the signs of God's presence? And shouldn't I expect better developments to write about? Our story was getting worse instead of better!

Still, I had to remember that the Lord had provided me with Patti's help as He had provided Aaron for Moses. She had extensive writing experience (though she'd never written a book), and I once taught high school English. Together—with

God's help—we could do this.

While Moses had received God's promises of deliverance directly, I could hope in those same promises because Moses and I have the same God. I could read his words of confidence in God and take heart: "The Lord will fight for you; you need only to be still" (Exodus 14:13, 14).

God spoke to me more directly one night during the week after Nancy filed the Supreme Court petition. In a perfectly clear dream, Pat and I sat in a pew in an unfamiliar church while an unknown pastor stood at the front of our congregation. The pastor gave a benediction that solicited everyone's response.

"We know that suffering produces . . . "

"Perseverance!" we all replied.

"And perseverance produces . . . "

"Character!"

"And character produces . . . "

"Hope! And hope does not disappoint us."

Waking up, I recognized these words from the Bible but had no idea which book the passage came from. After finding the verses in Romans 5:3-5, I was amazed to realize that my subconscious mind could produce this, and to think that God could be speaking to me in my dreams in this way.

Psalm 16:7 says, "I will praise the Lord who counsels me; even at night my heart instructs me."

The proclamation of that dream thrilled me, especially ending with the promise that "hope does not disappoint us."

In my prayer time later that morning, I could say with the psalmist, "Remember your word to your servant for you have given me hope. My comfort in my suffering is this: Your promise preserves my life" (Psalm 119:49, 50).

I decided to write my own acronym in the margin of my

prayer journal: HOPE—Hinging On Prayer Expectantly.

In one of our eight-minute phone calls, Pat mentioned the arrival of a new inmate and asked if I would contact the man's wife. We prayed that I would have the right words to comfort Kristi, who lived within thirty minutes of our home and, like us, had two sons. The prison did not welcome camaraderie among the families on camp premises. But I needed every ounce of emotional support after Pat left home, and I now wanted to help another wife who found herself in my situation.

Kristi was thrilled that I reached out to her, and we both found solace through sharing our faith in the midst of mutual circumstances. She also let me know how much Pat was encouraging her husband. Kristi would later help me in a way I couldn't foresee.

In another phone call with Pat, he began telling me about playing basketball, which made me default to worrying about him. I feared that if he suffered an injury he would not receive adequate medical attention. On the other hand, I realized work-related exercise and team sports helped him manage stress. Pat promised to be careful, and I enjoyed hearing a bit of excitement in his voice.

"I got picked to be on a basketball team for a six-week league!"

"That's great, Pat. How did they select the teams?"

"Pretty much like recess on the playground. They chose two captains who picked us one at a time. I wasn't picked first, but I'm the only white guy on the team."

Hearing a chuckle in his voice made me smile.

Bastrop, like the rest of our country, was experiencing racial tension. Pat had previously told me how various groups segregated themselves in both their eating and television areas. Whites, blacks, and Hispanics did not mix at all.

I knew my husband was liked by all, and it made me proud of him for being chosen for that team.

In another conversation with Pat, I was the excited one.

"Pat! I'm so happy you're finally getting to tell your story of all the manipulative tactics used against you."

But my happiness only lasted until I awoke from a dream—so real—in which Pat was home again and had access to someone in authority.

At least the dream gave me hope that it could come true, maybe sooner than later. The unrelenting sting of injustice and the resulting life-twist it caused us seemed too hard to endure much longer.

In his devotion on Psalm 28, Tim Keller points out that David is our model for seeking God when we suffer from an injustice.

> He cries to God at the prospect of being unfairly charged and counted as a corrupt ruler. This is a major theme of the psalms, but not one that most of us in comfortable Western societies can easily understand. . . . Christians should also cry to God day and night against injustice (Luke 18:7).[3]

In between my bouts of crying to God day and night, I managed to do a few normal things. Just three days after that hopeful dream, my friend Kathy invited me to see a movie after work. Though I felt tired and despondent, I agreed to go.

The day of our outing happened to be "Fat Tuesday," the eve of Lent. Maybe that's why we decided to have dinner out after the movie. We drove for about ten minutes before changing our minds about where to eat. Kathy turned her car around, and we went all the way back to a Mexican restaurant next to the theater.

While the waiter placed chips and hot sauce on our table, I looked up and noticed a familiar person seated at the table directly across from me. The man in his mid-seventies did not know me, but I could not forget his face. This was the judge who sentenced Pat!

I became visibly upset and my heart began to race. When Kathy learned the reason, she began to pray, asking God to give me "peace in the midst" of this painful situation and a release from the judge's stronghold over me.

We could easily hear the judge sharing old school stories with friends. However, hearing his casual comments regarding court cases and convictions left us wide-eyed.

"Luann, don't you see he's a man just like anyone else?" Kathy asked.

"Yes, but he has inflicted so much pain on our family."

After we left the restaurant, I noticed a text sent from Maribel earlier in the day:

*Luann, in my spirit, I heard these words for you today. Starting this evening, you are to release any fears you have.*

Maribel had no idea about the encounter I just had. But the Holy Spirit did.

At home, I phoned Patti to tell her about my "chance meeting." She suspected what I was about to say even before I could finish.

Patti reminded me that several times in recent weeks, I had told her how I wanted to see the judge, to let him know Pat was innocent. Now, as I told her about seeing him—even though he never noticed me—Patti remembered something else.

"Luann! Oh . . . do you know what's coming next in *The Songs of Jesus*? I'm pretty sure . . . "

"Are you telling me it's Psalm 23?"

Phone in hand, we each hurried to grab our copy of the new devotional book.

I pulled my book open by the ribbon that marked the next reading. There it was, the familiar psalm with the incredible words of verse five: "You prepare a table before me in the presence of my enemies."

Amazed, I went on to read the study section.

> PEACE IN THE MIDST. God has a celebration meal with us not after we finally get out of the dark valley but in the middle of it, in the presence of our enemies. He wants us to rejoice in him in the midst of our troubles. Is our shepherd out of touch with reality? Hardly. . . . He understands what we are going through and will be with us every step of the way.[4]

Psalm 23 materialized after both of my encounters with the prosecutor, and now after seeing the judge. Three times! The psalm had appeared unexpectedly each time from a different reading source.

As I stood staring at the page, I also noticed the title, with every letter capitalized: PEACE IN THE MIDST. The phrase repeated the exact words Kathy had prayed for me at the restaurant.

My limited phone time with Pat would be too brief to tell him all that had happened. I saved the story of God's fresh encouragement until I could share the amazing details face-to-face.

Pat and I chose a hard, cold bench over indoor chaos for our next visit. When I finished recounting the series of events, a male cardinal swooped down beside us—as if to confirm my story by adding an exclamation point in red. The bird landed in the pine straw beside our table and paused in that familiar way we'd begun to interpret as a silent message: *Yes, God is watching over you.*

Could this be coincidental? Hardly! We believed that God indeed understood what we were going through and that He was with us every step of the way.

# Chapter 18

# Kicked Around
# Long Enough

*When I am afraid, I will trust in you.*
PSALM 56:3

We knew the Supreme Court appeal was a long shot. Even so, we believed nothing was too difficult for our God. However, bad news came exactly one month from the night of that dinner "in the presence of" my enemy.

Pat's call came earlier than usual on this evening, and I knew from his voice that something was wrong.

"Luann, Nancy just called me. Our appeal was denied." He paused before he could continue. "I don't know what to do."

My heart began to pound as I reeled from this latest punch. Adding to our pain, the limited, seven-minute conversation allowed little time for consolation. Since Andrew had gone out for dinner, I sat alone in numb silence, until the phone rang again: Alan.

"Mom, I'm really concerned about Andrew. He tries to hold everything in, but I know he's not doing well."

This new worry added to my pain. I hurt—physically—for Andrew, for Pat, for all of us. But how could I encourage Andrew to trust God for the future when I struggled with this myself?

I couldn't even pray that night. I now faced the private burden of trying to protect the others from additional concern. Though I had shared the latest edition of bad news with Alan, I purposely did not inform Andrew yet. I also decided to spare Pat the news of Andrew's depression over our circumstances.

How could we go forward with any hope of a secure future with that final door slammed in our face? We must have been gullible to think justice could come from a self-serving system that repeatedly denies innocent victims. We felt betrayed by our own country. This was not the land of "liberty and justice for all" we had believed in.

Before heading to work the next morning, I poured a cup of coffee for my devotional time and wrote this urgent prayer in my journal:

*Are we to stand and watch You fight, or are You going to direct us to fight by other means? Please reveal this to us with clarity. Please be near Pat and Andrew right now.*

Still holding my journal, I noticed the Bible verses I'd recorded the day before, only eight hours before our hopes were crushed: "Do not be afraid of any man, for judgment belongs to God. . . . The Lord your God, who is going before you, will fight for you, as he did for you in Egypt, before your very eyes" (Deuteronomy 1:17, 30).

I believed God provided those verses as an answer for me before I had even formed the words of my prayer. He would go before us and fight for us. I reminded myself of the lesson from my unbelievable encounter with the judge: not to fear any man nor forget the things my eyes had seen.

In suffering we can either run to God or away from Him. I was learning to run to God's Word because I knew He would meet me there. Like a pilot flying in dense fog who must rely on his instruments, I needed to trust God to guide us even though I saw no landing strip on my radar. His promises soothed my anxieties: He will never forsake us (Deuteronomy 31:6); He will lead us to green pastures (Psalm 23:2); He will protect us from trouble and surround us with songs of deliverance (Psalm 32:7).

Still distraught over the denied appeal, I began recording Jeremiah 31:25 in my journal each morning: "I will refresh the weary and satisfy the faint." Though I didn't know how God would do this, I had experienced his refreshing countless times throughout our ordeal.

Nancy, too, was distressed over our failure to receive justice. She had one last-ditch effort to recommend. She told us about a "2255" motion we could file to address insufficient legal representation by one member of our original legal team.

We had little strength—and no more funds—for another legal battle. Yet, having any option other than surrender would at least give us a more positive focus.

I continued to visit Pat every weekend, but now without the hope of his sudden, early release. To fortify my spirit on the drive to Bastrop, I played a certain Stephen Curtis Chapman song over and over again. With gusto, I sang along to "Hallelujah, You Are Good." The lyrics speak of trusting God in times of despair even when we cannot feel His presence. The words of truth ministered to my soul.

During this time of deep disappointment, something unexpected lifted my spirit. I actually began waking up with praise songs running through my mind. I experienced the truth of Psalm 42:8: "By day the Lord directs his love, at night his song is with me—a prayer to the God of my life."

Even though I continually steeped myself in the reassurance of God's Word, I struggled to get through each day. Friends tried to cheer me by inviting me to go out with them. But I could not pretend to be well, and I did not want to pull them down. I was too exhausted to go out and play.

I did play my piano, however. My weekly lessons felt therapeutic—a healthy and relaxing escape from the madness of the circumstances. My piano teacher gave me apropos words during one session: "Luann, the composer included rests in this piece, and they are just as important to the melody as the notes."

I had trouble implementing the rests in musical manuscripts. As long as the notes continued to flow, I played along, but those rests would trip me up. I also stumbled over the "accidentals," the notes that do not follow the key signature. But I learned that musical pieces with rests and accidentals provide a more complex melody, one with depth and emotion.

Practicing the piano seemed to reflect my personal life. I found it hard to insert any rest, and my days followed no key signature—no clear course. I could only hope our pain and loss would turn into something good and yield some beauty from the ashes.

My visits with Pat became more difficult in the weeks after our third failed attempt at justice. Neither of us could manage to console the other. One Sunday, we felt desperate for cheer as we sat outside by ourselves. We actually bowed our heads in prayer and asked God to send a cardinal our way. When we looked up, we beheld this bird in all its red glory as it perched in the tree beside us. Our tears of appreciation fell together on the picnic table as we marveled over a loving God so very present in our trouble.

Further encouragement came during this same visit. Three inmates at separate times approached me with their families to say how much Pat meant to them. They said Pat kept them going and his faith in Christ overflowed in all he did. One man mentioned how he loved seeing Pat pray with me over the phone each night. Their words affirmed that God could indeed use our bad circumstances to influence others for good.

Cardinals and comforting words helped like a medicine, restoring my peace for hours or even a day before the arrival of some new attack on my well-being. Evil now presented itself in the form of threatening letters. The IRS wanted its percentage of our seized income.

Although the government continued to take 100 percent of Pat's commission-based earnings, our tax agent had to report the garnished wages as "income" for Pat. As a result, the IRS now claimed we owed taxes on wages Pat never received—not one penny.

In response to that threat, Nancy requested a release of the money held in the court registry—Pat's confiscated funds—to pay those taxes. The judge denied this request. It seemed the government—like the cruel Pharaoh of Moses' day—decided we could gather our own straw to make bricks to build the empire.

In hysteria over the arrival of still another IRS letter one day, I called Patti. As I read the threatening statements to her, she recalled a Bible story of another troubling letter.

King Hezekiah of Judah trusted in God but also feared the Assyrians, who had already laid waste some of Judah's fortified cities and taken much silver and gold from Hezekiah. The king tore his clothes and put on sackcloth (2 Kings 19:1). But the Assyrian army commander, Sennacherib, kept returning and threatening to destroy Judah unless the people surrendered everything. God would not be able to help them, according to Sennacherib, who sent messengers with a final threat (2 Kings 19:9-13). However, the king did not panic.

> Hezekiah received the letter from the messengers and read it. Then he went up to the temple of the Lord and spread it out before the Lord. And Hezekiah prayed . . . . "Give ear, O Lord, and hear; open your eyes, O Lord, and see . . . deliver us from his hand, so that all kingdoms on earth may know that you alone, O Lord, are God" (2 Kings 19:14-16, 19).

I had no altar, but I put the IRS letters in my Bible to remind me to trust God with these threats. Even so, I felt bullied to the bone and gripped by fear. In my daily journal, along with recording Jeremiah 31:25, I added 2 Timothy 1:7: "For God has not given us a spirit of fear, but of power and of love and of a sound mind" (NKJV). I was no poster child for this verse, but I wanted to believe God's Word above my feelings.

In *Songs of Jesus* I read timely words: "Fearfulness and faith in God can coexist in us even as trust slowly wins out. Faith is not a vague sense that 'God will work it out.' It comes from prayerful immersion in the Scripture."[1]

My deeper times in personal Bible study served to remind me that: God does allow evil; good people are not exempt from troubles; and God's rewards for faithfulness are assured only in the next life.

The psalms especially reveal that followers of God suffered injustice and cried out to God even while trusting Him. *The Message* version of the Bible expresses suffering in words I understood all too well.

> We're watching and waiting, holding our breath, awaiting your word of mercy. Mercy, God, mercy! We've been kicked around long enough . . . kicked when we're down by arrogant brutes (Psalm 123).[2]

> God, get me out of here, away from this evil; protect me from these vicious people . . . Stuffed with self-importance, they plot ways to trip me up, determined to bring me down (Psalm 140).[3]

Along with referring us to a new attorney for the possible legal motion, Nancy arranged for a CPA to help with the complexity of our tax situation. I dreaded meeting this man without Pat to do the speaking, but as I walked into "Mr. B's" office, his kind demeanor helped me relax.

I also noticed a familiar college diploma on the wall. Mr. B had graduated from Stephen F. Austin State University—Pat's and my alma mater. This small piece of information put me further at ease. I also learned he was trained in classical music on the piano. The two of us discussed Chopin before turning our attention to taxes.

Mr. B planned to file motions to protect us from the impossible tax demands against us. But he warned that the IRS can be quite aggressive. "You should keep an eye on your bank accounts," he told me.

At home, another situation pressed in on me. Andrew had been wanting his own dog for some time, and he didn't want to wait any longer. As he reasoned, "A puppy would provide a healthy distraction and bring some life into our house."

I had to agree that our home felt empty without Pat. Life now revolved around our jobs and visits to Bastrop. The ongoing circumstances had obviously affected Andrew's life too, and I lamented that his plans for his own apartment had been on hold since graduation. But the last thing I needed was another dog!

Still, watching my son's excitement as he studied various breeds led me to begin searching the Internet along with him. We reached a mutual conclusion after finding an adorable litter of Goldendoodle puppies—one was still available. Puppy number seven, born in North Texas, would be ready for a new home by early summer.

Andrew and I made a travel plan for the first weekend of June. We would drive to Austin, stay with Alan and Alix, and then my sons and I would continue to North Texas to claim the little bundle of joy. Happy for Andrew, I actually grew excited. Surely the world could not be all wrong when we had a puppy to hold and enjoy.

When the anticipated Friday afternoon arrived, I stopped by the bank after work to deposit my paycheck before leaving town. At home, while packing my overnight bag, I thought to check my bank balance online, something I rarely did. I soon found myself staring at the computer screen in disbelief. The money in my account had been withdrawn—all of it!

My entire body began to shake. With trembling hands, I called our troops for prayer and help. I also had the presence of mind to call my employer hoping he could stop payment on the paycheck I had just deposited. I purposely did not tell Pat since I knew this news would devastate him. It could wait until I saw him on Sunday.

This day that began purposeful—even joyful—turned sober for both Andrew and me. Even so, we went through the motions in order to keep our plans intact. It may have helped that I was in shock, not yet absorbing the impact of this latest dagger. Andrew calmly loaded my car, and we left for Austin as planned. Sensing my distress, he turned on soothing praise music for the drive.

Early Saturday morning, after a sleepless night, we embarked on a six-hour round trip. As Alan drove, my reality began to sink in, or perhaps I began to sink into reality. I was gripped by fear and could not stop crying as my mind reeled with unanswered questions. How could so much injustice persist? Where was God in all of this?

This latest blow seemed both wrong and cruel. The judge had previously said I could keep the funds left to me by my late parents since all of my joint savings and investments with Pat had been taken. Yet the IRS seized my account without notice, taking all of my inheritance money—all I had left to live on. I further lost my freshly deposited paycheck—a month's salary.

Besides paying household bills with my personal account, I had also paid our property taxes. We had never missed a tax payment of any kind in more than thirty years. But the IRS now demanded 38 percent of Pat's 100-percent-confiscated income.

How could anyone be expected to pay taxes on income never received?

I saw the irony of picking up a puppy on that "Frodo Friday" since it proved to be a helpful diversion that likely kept me from falling headlong into despair. I found myself grateful that Andrew wouldn't have to deliberate over which puppy to choose since he already expected to receive the "last pick of the litter." As we headed back to Austin, it soothed my spirit to see little Riggins nestled in Andrew's arms.

The next day, even a soothed spirit could not mask my soul's agony as I arrived at the Bastrop camp. I couldn't hold back tears as I delivered the latest blow to Pat. The wretched facts of my drained account left us both bewildered and bereft. We could only pray for God to show us what to do next.

Many friends and family members stepped in during the next few days to help in various ways. Some met with our attorneys and decided to help with legal fees. Others spent extended time with me. One friend sent weekly meal kits that relieved my shopping and dinner planning. Another friend took me for a needed doctor visit. And everyone continued to pray for us.

In July, at my lowest point, Dee Dee took me to meet a husband-wife ministry team who would pray for me. These former missionaries to India laid their hands on my shoulders and took turns praying.

Instead of crying—my default response now—I found myself smiling and almost radiant, which felt supernatural. The afterglow of their prayers remained with me.

Within days, something else touched my spirit when a friend told me to read the book of Obadiah. Unfamiliar with this minor prophet whose book is the shortest in the Old Testament, I looked it up in my Bible. I read the words of God's judgment against those who showed no mercy to His people. While I read the commentary on Obadiah, my heart quickened: "We can be confident in God's final victory. He is our champion, and we can trust him to bring about true justice."[4]

Though trusting God for our future, we couldn't grasp the enormity of the ongoing injustices. Yet we could hold to the tangible encouragements He sent us through the kind deeds and sacrifices of those who cared for us.

The enduring summer heat added a physical drain to the emotional ones. However, we now had something substantial to look forward to: Pat would be leaving Bastrop by the end of summer.

Pat's ever-true friend Mitch had single-handedly completed necessary paperwork that demonstrated proof of a viable job as required by the federal prison board for possible early release. Like everyone else in the prison system, Pat would be required to spend at least several weeks of transition in a halfway house before coming home.

After two long years, we could finally count down Pat's remaining days away from us.

## Chapter 19

# As Right as Wrong Can Be

*However, I consider my life worth nothing to me,*
*if only I may finish the race and complete the task*
*the Lord Jesus has given me—the task of testifying*
*to the gospel of God's grace.*

Acts 20:24

Storm clouds darkened the sky on a Monday morning in
August as I loaded my car for the final trip to Bastrop. The
hot, sticky atmosphere seemed ominous, as if ready to burst—
matching my nervous state. After experiencing so many
snafus at the hand of the federal government, I worried that
something might go wrong with Pat's departure. Thankfully,
Andrew did the driving.

Upon our arrival at the camp's administrative office, I was
told to wait outside—in the rain. I chose to sit in the car with
Andrew and field incoming phone calls from Alan, Kenny,
and Pat's mom, all of whom anxiously waited for Pat's release.

The tension in our family had been mounting for six days because the camp prematurely cut off Pat's ability to communicate with us.

The camp staff tested our patience with another two hours of waiting that morning. When Pat finally emerged from the building, instead of heading toward our car, he assisted another departing inmate. Without an umbrella, Pat became soaking wet as he carried the man's boxes to his car.

"Well, of course," Andrew said. "It's Dad's last day here, and he's helping someone else."

When Pat was safely inside our car, the three of us cried together for a few minutes before he phoned family members. One call was especially timely.

"Happy birthday, Mom!"

"Oh, Pat. This is the best birthday present ever—just knowing you're leaving that dreadful place." Linda's relief equaled ours.

The rain intensified and threatened a delay as we drove back to San Antonio. Though we desperately wanted to go straight home, we had orders to deliver Pat straight to his assigned halfway house on the opposite side of the city.

For at least eight weeks, Pat would have to endure "assistance" in a classroom filled with repeat drug offenders who needed instruction on how to become contributing members of society. If only the authorities knew the man we knew: Sunday school teacher, youth and community leader, coach, inner-city missions volunteer, faithful friend, neighbor, godly husband and father.

I was grateful to have seen the facility the week before, thanks to Kristi, whose husband had been released from prison several months earlier and assigned to this same place. She reassured me how much better things would be for Pat and me once he was back in San Antonio, even though he would not be home. Best of all, he'd have a cell phone without time restrictions. No more anxious and rushed evening conversations!

We entered the halfway house—a former convent—with high hopes. It offered private rooms, a dining hall, a library, and spacious grounds.

"Hello, Mr. Mire. We have been expecting you. However, you've been reassigned to a different location. You're going to the Hall House." The man spoke in a matter-of-fact manner, without apology.

Pat, so accustomed to institutional red tape and confusion, accepted this glitch in silence. But I piped up: "Why?"

The man explained this halfway house was at capacity, but assured us Pat would be fine.

I wasn't so sure. This was not the plan!

We left that old brick building with its life-size statue of Jesus and made our way to Hall House, a small, corrugated-steel building sandwiched between busy railroad tracks and a noisy interstate. Finding no parking lot, we pulled close to the curb and waded across a now flooded street to check in.

The Hall House administrator showed kindness in welcoming Pat, but he informed us that his facility also was full. Further, we learned that all residents—around thirty men—slept in bunks in one large room. There was no kitchen; all meals were delivered by a food service company. There was no library either; all residents shared one computer in a noisy TV room. And there were no spacious grounds.

Maybe the man's compassionate manner helped us digest the disappointments about this reassignment. Pat and I both had an unexpected sense of peace even though, by comparison, the first facility offered luxurious accommodations.

Andrew shared our peace and offered a positive outlook. "Dad," he asked, "how could you help anyone if you were in a private room?"

Pat's first privilege soon came: Andrew and I could pick up dinner for him. We chose a nearby fast-food restaurant that offered selections he had not tasted in two years—a cheeseburger, fries, and a strawberry shake.

A happy surprise interrupted Pat's meal. Alan had driven from Austin to join our celebration, and his gift of humor put us all at ease in the new surroundings.

Leaving Pat at the bare-bones, crowded facility that evening was at least a clear improvement over saying goodbye to him every Sunday at Bastrop. Besides, we were too tired at the end of our long day to be emotional. We parted with the knowledge that he was now in San Antonio and only a phone call away—24/7.

Within forty-eight hours of his arrival at Hall House, Pat received permission to begin working. And he had the perfect job lined up! Dee Dee and the board of directors at Blueprint Ministries offered him temporary employment as an assistant for construction projects.

In the past, Pat had both volunteered for and financially supported Blueprint. It now seemed providential that the charitable organization's downtown headquarters was a mere ten-minute drive from the halfway house. This proximity would prove to be a great help to us since residents were not allowed to drive.

Mitch, always willing to go the extra mile, offered to drive Pat to work on the first day. He arrived with breakfast tacos and donuts—just two more items on the long list of ways he continually encouraged Pat.

For lunch that day, I drove from my office to meet Pat at Blueprint. Our friends Scott and Tammy joined us and supplied take-out barbecue for a mini celebration. The four of us cried tears of joy.

Thus, the reunions began. For days, a friend or family member arrived at Blueprint to visit with Pat during lunch.

My new routine involved picking up Pat by 7:45 a.m. each weekday to take him to work before commuting to my workplace. This "Uber-Lu" role meant an extra hour or more in heavy traffic, but I was so happy to see Pat every morning. Dee Dee and others helped me by taking turns driving him back to the halfway house.

Though blessings kept coming, nothing was simple during this phase. When Pat received permission to attend worship services, his choices were limited to those on a list of preapproved churches in the vicinity of Hall House. And he couldn't just slip in casually to join the congregation. The powers that be required Pat to call upon arrival at church and then again before leaving the premises.

We chose First Baptist Church of San Antonio for our first Sunday of freedom. We personally knew one couple connected to this large downtown church. After stopping by the church office before the service to make the required phone call, Pat heard a familiar voice.

"Pat, is that you? I can't believe you're here! We've been praying for you!" Brian, the associate pastor, was married to one of Pat's childhood friends and knew about our circumstances. His warm welcome seemed like the arms of God around us.

"I've only been in San Antonio for five days," Pat said. "It's so good to see you and to be in a church again."

As we sat in a pew waiting for the service to begin, I recalled several dreams during my years without Pat. In more than one of those, he and I sat together in a church pew I didn't recognize. Now, here we were, ready to worship in an unfamiliar sanctuary.

When Brian opened the service in prayer, Pat took my hand in his—our habit for the past thirty-two years. My world felt secure again.

After the service Pat and I decided on a picnic lunch at a dilapidated table in the weed-infested lot beside Hall House. Sadly, this "accommodation" seemed normal to us after so many visits spent in the sparse surroundings of the Bastrop camp. With those days now behind us, we ate our hamburgers almost blissfully. There were no shade trees to offer us the hope of seeing our favorite bird, but the Lord was not hindered by the setting. From a thicket of overgrown brush, a bright red cardinal emerged!

Three weeks passed before Pat received a four-hour pass to come home. We both cried with relief as he walked into our house. I wanted to enjoy each minute without burdening him with a "honey-do" list of things that needed his attention, both inside and out. But Pat couldn't wait to get started.

My husband was in his element as he walked around with tools to tackle the chores. And I was his happy wife again.

Pat fixed the sound system first, though I hadn't missed listening to music much while he'd been away. By the time Andrew arrived, music filled our house, along with the aroma of steaks cooking on the patio grill. His dad was home!

On the next weekend of Pat's visit, Alan and Alix came from Austin to join us. We all attended the "preapproved" church downtown; this service had become a weekly blessing for both Pat and me. As the pastor closed his sermon, he added an admonition: "Some of you have something you need to finish. Go and finish it."

Those words had clear meaning for me. I needed to get back to writing my story. The project I believed the Lord had given me stalled back in June with the seizure of my accounts. Pat's arrival in San Antonio at the end of August and my extra hours of driving and visiting him left me little available time or energy.

Life would gradually return to a more normal routine as Pat's privileges increased. In my devotion time on the morning of his first weekend at home, I read the Latin phrase Et Teneo, Et Teneor—"I hold and am held." I praised God for this truth.

Though I now had a smile on my face much of the time, I retained an undercurrent of pain due to the ongoing injustices that threatened our future. The government wasn't finished with us. Our lake house was the next item on their list to extract funds from us—to pay for the misdeeds of others.

I had long reminded myself that the lake house was only a possession, not a necessity to life or happiness. But it held warm memories of gatherings with family and friends over the years and fun times spent working side by side with Pat in remodeling. And now, with Pat still under travel restrictions of the halfway house, I would be required to go and witness the seizure of our property.

On the appointed day, Kenny and Wendye took off work, drove from Austin to pick me up, and then drove me to the lake house to stand by my side. The three of us arrived to find my uninvited guests: a representative of the prosecutor's office, their Realtor, and a federal marshal. The intimidating trio escorted us from room to room of my house.

As I tagged personal items we were allowed to keep, the marshal hovered nearby in accordance with government protocol—to protect their representatives during this "dangerous" procedure. I hoped the opposing team felt less threatened when they read Psalm 91:1 painted on the wall above our bed: "He who dwells in the shelter of the Most High will rest in the shadow of the Almighty."

In the den, I opened a cabinet door to remove old videos. These were recorded sermons from our former pastor that we enjoyed viewing as a family. When I mentioned wanting to keep them, the Realtor spoke up to say this same pastor had officiated at his wedding ceremony. I handed the man two of the videos to keep, hoping they would serve to testify to the character of our family.

Instead of agonizing over our loss that day, I was somehow able to pray for our "enemies"—those who invaded our sweet lake house. To keep from crying, I avoided looking out the back windows toward the beautiful lake, even though it would be my last opportunity.

Around this time, we also had to let go of another source of comfort that I would miss. Nancy had been our David who bravely hurled stones at Goliath. Though unable to slay the giant, she left some sharp stones beneath its feet. Nancy went well beyond the role of a legal advocate and allowed me to keep her on speed dial for two years. She also shared our bitter disbelief at the ongoing injustice we suffered.

Nancy confirmed our fears that it is very difficult to get justice with the federal government. The accused faces a federal prosecutor who works to convince a federal judge of wrongdoing. The prosecutor and judge are not only on the same side, they're often former coworkers.

As our battle against the government continued, Pat, more than anything else, wanted the judge to know the truth. Our best legal hope now focused on the 2255 filing. Pat's case qualified for this motion since the ruling against his appeal emphasized that his attorneys should have objected more on the day of sentencing. But taking this step would involve hiring another attorney. We found ourselves like so many others who keep fighting for justice: out of funds.

The government, of course, had plenty of resources, including our savings, retirement, investments, and now the lake house. We had nothing substantial left beyond our home. We also needed an attorney who specialized in restitution. Yet we could not be sure any legal effort would help us, and we were so tired of pushing against the ironclad doors of the justice system.

We received fresh encouragement and relief when friends Mitch and Bruce spearheaded the new legal effort by searching for an attorney skilled in the 2255. The "mighty men" who had already sacrificed their Saturdays to visit Pat for two years now stepped in and paid the preliminary fees.

These friends and others validated Tim Keller's words: "Suffering, rightly met, creates rich community and friendship."[1]

Despite all our troubles, we'd been truly blessed with faithful friends and family. How could we ever repay such kindness?

Pat's consecutive weekends at home arrived with the long-anticipated autumn weather, which seemed perfectly timed for much needed visits with our extended family. A late October weekend included my birthday, and though Pat's presence was clearly my gift, he made me feel like a princess—at least until I returned my Prince Charming to his halfway house. But now we could count the days until mid-November, when he could come home to stay.

That day finally arrived, but Pat's homecoming, as we discovered, became more like home confinement. Though he regained his driving privileges, he had to call Hall House every time he left home for work, call them again when he arrived at Blueprint, and yet again before heading home. And he couldn't make any stops between work and home.

The halfway house staff called Pat too—every night. They called after ten o'clock to make sure he was home. They checked on him again during the wee hours of the morning. These calls grated on our nerves, yet we were too grateful to be together to let it bother us much.

With Pat living at home again, we could now worship at our local church. However, since I'd spent each Sunday in Bastrop during the last two years, I had attended a church that offered Saturday night services. Oak Hills Church met my needs both practically and spiritually, and it would also serve as our place of worship in this transition time. And unlike our small church that met in a middle school auditorium, this megachurch had an office phone—still required during Pat's ongoing probation period.

Max Lucado, the pastor at Oak Hills, had ministered to me time and again through both his books and preaching as I battled fear and anxiety during Pat's absence. Now, with my husband beside me, I listened to the pastor's message less desperately.

During one Sunday sermon, I found myself holding an internal conversation with God about my book project—once again in pause mode. I even doodled some words of frustration on the church bulletin: *I'm not a writer or a theologian.* But the pastor soon regained my full attention.

"Your words have power," Lucado told the congregation. "You can be your own worst critic or your greatest cheerleader. You can disagree with God's plan for your life and agree with the devil, or tell the devil to get lost."[2]

Had the Lord just addressed my freshly made excuse? I did not want to "agree with the devil" about my inadequacies. The admonition encouraged me to get back to work on my story. I became determined, like the apostle Paul, to "finish the race and complete the task the Lord Jesus has given me—the task of testifying to the gospel of God's grace" (Acts 20:24).

The Thanksgiving holiday arrived at the perfect time for our first family gathering at home in almost three years. Since most of our extended family members came to celebrate with us, it meant that fourteen people and their pets—four dogs and a cat—slept all over the place!

Along with the dogs running in circles around us, our home was filled with favorite foods, fall décor, games, and laughter. Wayne and Clare came from across the street to join our feast, which served as a fitting occasion for us to offer heartfelt thanks and praise to God.

Since Pat's probation prevented out-of-town travel beyond a restricted area, our family members planned to be with us again for Christmas. I couldn't wait to "deck the halls" to usher in the festive Yuletide season. I pulled out boxes of lights, ornaments, nativities, and all things Christmas.

On the morning of Christmas Eve, I served a holiday brunch before our extended family went to worship at Oak Hills. Sitting in the sanctuary between Pat and his brother, I reflected on the many occasions Kenny had stepped in to serve as his brother's keeper. Tears of gratitude and relief streamed down my face.

Christmas Day featured a smoked turkey sent by friends to supply our full house, and I added the trimmings: cornbread dressing, butternut squash, green beans with Madeira sauce, green salad, cherry compote, and lemon cake. I happily went overboard for this very merry Christmas.

In January, while Pat continued to work at Blueprint Ministries, he began to make contacts in the hope of restarting his career. But his driving restrictions and those intrusive nighttime phone calls reminded us that our lives were not quite back to normal.

Meanwhile, Andrew made plans that would help him return to normal. Pat and I assured our son his life had been on hold long enough. We were excited to see his enthusiasm about moving into a house across town with two friends from college.

Just a few weeks into the new year, while Pat deliberated the pros and cons concerning the 2255, I heard familiar chirping. I went outside looking around for a redbird, which I had not seen in several months. Seeing nothing, I said, "I hear you, but I can't see you." Within a minute, a single male cardinal flew right past my face. I yelled, "There you are!"

In my spirit, I uttered a prayer. *And here I am, Lord. Forgive me for not always seeing that you are with me. Thank you for your presence whether or not I see you.*

The date to file the 2255 came on February 28. With much angst, Pat decided to relinquish what appeared to be his last legal option. Though he still wanted the judge to hear his story, Pat had heard from multiple sources that the judge did not want to deal with his case any further.

February 28 also happened to be "Fat Tuesday." This red-letter day at least brought something good. The more difficult stage of Pat's probation had come to an end—no more intrusive phone calls or travel restrictions. So, instead of bemoaning the fact of another closed door, Pat and I chose to get away from it all. We drove to Austin.

As we joined Alan and Alix for dinner that night, I considered the irony of this Tuesday before Lent. The judge who once again thwarted our hopes was the same man I encountered at the Mexican restaurant exactly one year ago.

We needed to keep our perfect Judge in mind, and his words. "'For I know the plans I have for you,' declares the Lord, 'plans to prosper you and not to harm you, plans to give you hope and a future'" (Jeremiah 29:11).

Meanwhile, I had one happy plan to preoccupy me in a positive way. With Pat's March birthday three weeks away, I wanted to celebrate. It was time for the tambourines!

# Chapter 20

# Dancing and Singing

*You turned my wailing into dancing: you removed my sackcloth and clothed me with joy, that my heart may sing to you and not be silent. O Lord my God, I will give you thanks forever.*

Psalm 30:11, 12

Reaching to the top shelf of the coat closet, I pulled down the two boxes of small tambourines I ordered in the early days of Pat's appeal, when I hoped to plan a celebration. But later, in bitter disappointment over the repeated denials from the courts, I had hidden them from view, thinking I'd been a fool to hope for justice.

Seeing these party favors reminded me of what I once thought victory would look like. I now realized we still had plenty to celebrate. And Pat's approaching birthday in March would provide the perfect opportunity to mark his new beginning while surrounded by family and friends.

Though Pat was reluctant about all the attention on him, I knew the gathering in our home would be important. The party I had in mind would center around thankfulness to God.

A friend of Alan's helped me select songs of praise for the event, and she also agreed to play the piano and lead our time of worship. Other friends, including Patti, who'd had a close-up view of our suffering, said they'd be honored to share their thoughts about the goodness of God they had witnessed.

The evening would also include a brief communion service led by Dee Dee. Since we had missed this observance as a family, I wanted to honor the presence of Christ, whose nearness in our trouble kept us from being crushed.

Besides enjoying a light dinner with our guests, each of those simple but profound acts would constitute our celebration.

My sister-in-law, Wendye, became my willing assistant. Together, we designed and mailed the party invitations and planned a menu. Despite all of my doubts about the tambourines, these became Pinterest-worthy after we made silver-leafed insets to cover the pastel centers. Our glammed-up party favors now matched the invitations, but they also included the words of Jeremiah 31:4: "Again, you will take up your tambourine and go out and dance with the joyful."

When the week of the party arrived, my regular blessings list began to write itself. However, the first item was unexpected; Pat needed my help due to a scheduling conflict at Blueprint Ministries. So, instead of preparing for his party after arriving home from work each evening, I joined him to serve dinner to a group of out-of-town high school students who volunteered to spend their spring break working with

Blueprint to repair homes around San Antonio.

That unexpected request later seemed like divine intervention because we served the meals at our former church—the one we'd left with a heavy heart a few years back. It lifted my spirit to be in the familiar kitchen again and know our former church had offered to house the students during their mission trip.

It further blessed me to serve alongside some of the friends who had faithfully visited Pat in Bastrop for two years. Several of these men and their wives had, like us, joined other congregations in recent years. Now, for this one week, we served as the body of Christ together again—with laughter, pranks, prayers, and praises to God.

Although I would not have picked the timing of that service opportunity, it allowed me to revisit an important chapter of my life that needed some better closing lines.

Another unexpected "opportunity" arrived the night before Pat's party. Since Alan and Alix decided to arrive early that evening, Andrew invited the four of us to go out to a dance hall after dinner because his roommate's band would be playing. This idea seemed crazy, especially going out after nine o'clock—my bedtime. But Pat and I had always enjoyed dancing, and we couldn't pass up this fun opportunity.

I ended up dancing every song with either Pat or one of my sons. Again, we spent the evening laughing, like normal people. However, going to bed at one-thirty in the morning was not normal!

I woke up Friday morning from my abbreviated hours of sleep knowing I had to prepare for the eighty guests coming to our party that evening. I anticipated an early arrival for many of them—some from out of town, and other local friends who planned to help with preparations.

All of this should have caused me stress, but instead I couldn't stop smiling. I was in fullness-of-joy mode and wanted to stay that way.

Though busy all day, I somehow tapped into reserve energy. By evening, my tired body forgot itself as I beheld the faces of longtime friends who filled our home. Each had supported us through prayers and deeds. One of them, Joyce, had written and mailed cards of encouragement to both Pat and me—every week for twenty-five months!

While family members manned the food trays from kitchen to dining room and back again, clusters of friends stood or sat in every available space. And no one looked sad anymore.

One friend standing near a backyard window called out to me in an excited voice: "Luann! Look in that tree by the patio. A cardinal is here to celebrate with you."

While work and party planning occupied my days for several weeks, Pat began easing back into familiar routines. Now that he could drive again—whenever and wherever—he wanted to rejoin his weekly Bible study with the same eight men who'd studied together for more than fifteen years.

After his first Thursday morning with that group in two years, Pat called me as I drove to work.

"You won't believe what we discussed today!"

Pat explained they nearly ran out of time for the actual study because the men were so eager to talk with him. The group leader eventually pulled them back to their focus, saying, "Let's just spend ten minutes on our topic for today, Nicodemus."

Pat knew all about Nicodemus! After his introduction to prison with thirteen days in solitary confinement, Pat had been transferred to the county detention center for a temporary stay before his move to the Bastrop prison. While he waited for his floor assignment that night, a visiting pastor offered him a one-on-one Bible discussion on Nicodemus, a member of the Jewish ruling council who sought out Jesus.

Then, after his arrival at Bastrop, Pat's first Bible lesson centered on Nicodemus, who defended Jesus before the Pharisees by asking a question Pat understood too well: "Does our law condemn anyone without first hearing him to find out what he is doing?" (John 7:51).

Circling back to Nicodemus during Pat's first week of freedom encouraged him. Maybe someday—somehow—he would get to share his story, which the judge never heard.

Like Pat, I wanted to resume attending a group Bible study. Though I understood there are different seasons in life, I wondered why I had to miss out on something so worthwhile. However, around the same time Pat returned to his men's group, the CEO at my workplace asked if I would be willing to lead a brief morning Bible study at the office once a week.

I felt apprehensive about the vulnerability of a spiritual opportunity in my workplace, which might lead to sharing personal struggles I preferred to keep to myself. But I accepted.

After praying about what materials to use, I suggested a devotional study booklet, *Our Daily Bread,* which had provided solid nourishment for Pat and me while he was away. A coworker who showed interest in the office study mentioned she'd thought of the same booklet. Confirmation! Our twenty-minute meeting on Wednesday mornings would include a Scripture reading, prayer, and thanksgiving.

I felt God's Spirit showing me that I could serve Him in the workplace as well as the church or community. And, once again, I noticed the return of another part of life I'd missed.

The weekend after Pat's party, our friend Lynn called to ask if we could join her at Oak Hills Church on Sunday morning. She'd heard that Steven Curtis Chapman—the Christian music artist whose lyrics had been so meaningful to me the last two years—would be leading worship, unannounced.

Lynn arrived at church early that morning and saved front row seats for us. While Pat and I waited for the service to begin, I noticed someone I hadn't seen in nearly eight months. I grabbed Pat's hand, knowing I had to introduce him to the woman who'd prayed for me at my lowest point.

"Eileen, do you remember me?" I asked. "I'm the one Dee Dee brought to you for prayer last summer at my lowest point. And this is my husband, Pat!"

"Luann, what a miracle! And you look absolutely radiant."

Seeing Eileen again was only the first blessing that day.

The pastor told the congregation Chapman was in town to introduce his recently published autobiography, which includes many personal struggles through his life. But Chapman came to share a song with the worshippers as well.

My tears started with the first notes of the familiar song. I couldn't believe it! Of all the titles Chapman could have chosen, he'd picked *my* song—the one I'd played and sung along with over and over again on the drive to Bastrop.

The song, "Hallelujah, You Are Good," had continually

reminded me that in our time of sorrow and fear we can still trust in God's great love. Now, in the recovery stage of those painful years, I could smile with the assurance of this truth.

When the service ended, I noticed Eileen standing at the altar to serve as a prayer partner for anyone in need. Pat and I sought her out again, and we experienced the warmth of God's love as Eileen placed her hands on our shoulders to give thanks for His grace to us. When her prayer ended, Pat rested his hand on Eileen's shoulder and prayed for her.

While Pat looked for full-time employment opportunities, several of his faithful Bastrop visitors provided part-time work. Perry and Tyler asked Pat to help them with their joint contracting business, and Jeff offered a consulting role for his supply company.

Good things seemed to be coming in a steady stream.

Pat's mighty men, with Jesse in the lead this time, pulled together financial support for our continuing legal expenses. Their efforts helped Pat continue to pay for a tax attorney recommended by Nancy to address the overreaching claims of both the court and the IRS.

In early May, the tax attorney called with positive news. A federal prosecutor assigned to resolve our tax dispute wanted to meet with us.

When Pat picked me up at work the day of our scheduled meeting with this prosecutor, we randomly turned onto a road that would take us in the right direction. We soon found ourselves following a "color guard." A pair of cardinals flew above our windshield as if they wanted to share this occasion with us!

Pat was especially amazed. "Luann, did you just see that? I can't believe it! This makes me feel like God is going before us."

The sight of those particular birds on this particular day and time offered hope for a positive outcome. It gave us a strong sense of peace despite our long string of defeats.

Sure enough, we finally received a reversal in our favor!

In the meeting, our attorney successfully convinced the government of its wrongdoing on that fateful Frodo Friday a year earlier when the IRS seized my personal funds. The prosecutor now agreed that the court registry should have paid out the taxes due on Pat's commission income, which the government had been collecting—in total—ever since Pat's unjust conviction. Though the admission would not help us recover my funds, it would remove the threat of an unbearable tax burden.

Further, the meeting ended with an agreement that assured us the government would not seize additional future earnings.

These important victories allowed us to move forward.

When Pat's restrictions ended, we returned to the church plant we had joined before our world fell apart. Though both of the larger churches we had attended during his months of probation served to bless and encourage us, we were excited about resuming fellowship with close friends at The Park Community Church. Right away, we joined a newly formed Sunday school class that included many of those who supported us through our journey.

Our thirty-third wedding anniversary came around in June, and we planned a three-day celebration to make up for the two occasions we had lost. We kicked it off by going out to dinner with Wayne and Clare, whose anniversary was the same week.

The following evening, we hosted our Sunday school class for a game night. When Pat surprised us with a champagne toast and a sweet poem he'd written for me, tears fell from the faces of several guests. Yet everyone was smiling.

We concluded our triple-treat celebration at the San Antonio Riverwalk, a romantic setting for any couple. After dinner, we enjoyed a performance by the local symphony orchestra, tickets courtesy of Wayne and Clare.

A few weeks later, a small incident reminded me of my Jesus-with-skin-on encounter at the beginning of our ordeal. Larry, the bookstore salesman I'd met several years earlier, said my husband sounded "simply perfect." This time, a stranger at a neighborhood restaurant offered similar words of affirmation.

While Pat and I enjoyed our pizza dinner that evening, an elderly woman next to us began to choke. After seeing she was no longer in danger, Pat got up to get a glass of water for her. That's when the woman's husband turned to me and said, "You are married to a good man. But I bet that is something you already know."

I did know it, but I relished hearing those words. My husband's reputation had been attacked and wounded. I wanted the whole world to know the virtues of the man I married.

Two other small but meaningful things struck me as God-incidents during the time of our restoration. These occurred back-to-back during the same church service.

On that Sunday, our pastor began leading the congregation through First Peter, the very book Pat and I had studied "together" when we were first apart, while he was in solitary confinement. The pastor reminded us of the characteristics of holiness described by Peter, who warned believers that holy living might well include suffering. Our pastor further challenged us to be faithful to Jesus Christ so that people will ask us the reason for our hope and we can offer an answer (1 Peter 3:15).

When the sermon ended, I could hardly believe my ears. The associate pastor began to offer a benediction by reading the exact Bible verses from my dream one year earlier, while Pat was still in prison. In that dream, Pat and I stood together in a church as a minister delivered a benediction straight from Romans 5:3-5. Now, we heard the same words spoken over us:

> " . . . we know that suffering produces perseverance; perseverance, character; and character, hope. And hope does not disappoint us, because God has poured out his love into our hearts by the Holy Spirit, whom he has given us."

The dream had been hopeful, but today's message provided real hope that only God could give. We knew He had brought us safely through the years that seemed to be wasted, and we could trust Him for whatever difficulties remained ahead.

In the beginning of our troubles, I viewed the evil circumstances as the biggest fight of our lives, and this was true. However, over time I began to see another aspect: it was also the biggest surrender of our lives.

I had begged God to deliver us from injustice so truth would win out. And I struggled to understand why God would allow suffering to continue for so long—for us and many other innocent people.

As we surrendered to God's purposes, we let go of the tight grip on our lives we'd held onto without realizing it. We experienced God's comfort when we acknowledged we were not in control. But we also needed to surrender again and again while we worked our way through the bitterness that continued to surface.

In the book *Things Not Seen,* author Jon Bloom asserts, "God is doing far more than we can see in our agonies. . . . The evil that causes your greatest misery will one day serve the omnipotent mercy of God, not only for you, but also for more people than you ever imagined."[1]

Or, as our friend's mother-in-law wanted us to know after Pat's sentencing, "Your afflictions are working for you."

I pray this will prove true in our circumstances, that all of our misery—our ashes—might someday be seen as something of beauty.

Looking back, I see that God was faithful to supply us with the strength we needed. His regular provisions included a hopeful verse or passage of Scripture, a comforting word from a friend, a neighbor's kind deed, a beautiful cardinal, a timely repetition, or a reassuring "coincidence."

All of these encouragements came to us like manna from Heaven. We couldn't store them up for the next day, but we didn't need to. God's compassion is "new every morning" (Lamentations 3:23).

Pat and I began to realize we did have a victory, though not as the world sees victory. God had not yet removed our problems or the evil that caused them, yet we benefited from His undeniable presence. God held us together in the most important ways: our faith, our marriage, our health, our family, and our friendships.

A friend offered a poignant remark when she joined Pat

and me for dinner one evening. With a smile, she said, "You have joy again. The Lord has restored your souls. Evil did not win."

Her words affirmed the verse I had read that week: "The word of God lives in you, and you have overcome the evil one" (1 John 2:14). They also alluded to Psalm 23, which I'd read by "coincidence" after each of my surprise encounters with the enemy—twice with the prosecutor, once with the judge. The first three verses of this psalm acknowledge God's faithfulness in bringing His sheep safely through danger: "The Lord is my shepherd, I shall not be in want. He makes me lie down in green pastures, he leads me beside quiet waters, he restores my soul . . . "

As I sat in my prayer chair early one morning. I heard a distinct chirping—so clear that it seemed to be in the room *with* me. I loved this particular bird-song I'd come to know as "cheer, cheer, cheer."

I had learned to recognize the sound of a cardinal among the competing noises of other birds. I likewise learned to distinguish God's voice among the clamor of other voices—fearful and confusing ones.

Pat soon interrupted my devotional time when he called out to me from the back door. I found him outside, pointing to the chimney, where a beautiful redbird stood, still chirping.

While I'd been sitting near the fireplace, the cardinal had perched as close as possible, right above me.

It seemed as if God wanted to remind us once again that He is with us—Immanuel.

He is here, here, *here*.

# Epilogue

The cardinals appear less frequently since Pat's return home. Maybe they have winged their way to others in need of encouragement. But God used one frantic redbird to speak to us both.

The trapped bird flapped his wings in a desperate attempt to free himself from the closed shutter of our garage window. We watched this beautiful male cardinal flutter in panic, unaware that his useless attempts only delayed our help. When the bird finally grew weary of his efforts, Pat pried open the slats, allowing him to fly away.

Seven years have passed since Pat's indictment. We've had our fair share of feeling trapped by our circumstances. However, like the bird, we have someone far more capable to free us. We only have to be still and let Him open any door according to His will.

What overwhelms us today often becomes part of God's plan for our restoration. Though we don't expect our past difficulties to exempt us from future suffering, we're better prepared when pain or loss comes our way again. Having experienced His goodness, we can trust that new blessings are in store—and sometimes just around the corner.

One of those surprise blessings came into our lives shortly after Pat's birthday party, when Andrew met a delightful young teacher and fellow A&M graduate named Kelsey. Only eight months later, I was planning another party—to celebrate their engagement!

In the weeks before Andrew and Kelsey's wedding day, Pat and I looked forward to another joyful life event. We joined Alix's parents in Austin, where we spent a sleepless night in and out of a hospital waiting room anticipating the arrival of our first grandchild. At 5 a.m., Alan came to escort us to Alix's room. I cried tears of joy when I saw our 6'2" son cradling his newborn in his arms. My heart overflowed as I held baby Anna—so beautiful, and named after my mother.

Midsummer brought joy upon joy. I saw it in Andrew's face as Kelsey walked down the aisle of an outdoor Texas Hill Country venue surrounded by a canopy of oak trees. I saw it in the faces of family members and friends who came to share our occasion; they saw the joy in my face as I twirled on the dance floor with my son. Once again, I felt like Cinderella—this time sweeping across the room in a beautiful evening gown instead of sweeping the patio.

During that first dance with Andrew, the sorrows of the years diminished with each line of the Steven Curtis Chapman song we'd chosen. "Glorious Unfolding" proclaims that life doesn't always turn out the way we thought it would, but we can hold on to God's promises. Those who trust in God find their story is not finished. Instead, they can expect a glorious revelation of His perfect plan.

# Acknowledgments

**To family and friends** mentioned in this book and those not included by name:

*Thank you for allowing me to share how you walked with me and often carried me on this difficult journey. Your constant prayers kept me afloat when the waves pounded against me. Thank you for encouraging me to stay the course.*

**To Patti Richter**, my writing partner, who navigated these uncharted waters with me:

*Every time I wanted to give up on the story, you gently reminded me of God's faithfulness. You always believed in me more than I believed in myself. With wise counsel and patience, you nudged me to persevere. Words cannot express my deep gratitude to you, as well as to your husband, Jim, who sacrificed family time so you could spend countless hours writing, rewriting, editing, listening, and praying with me.*

**To Pat**, who has been my anchor in this sea of darkness:

*Your unwavering faith has encouraged me to trust God in all circumstances. While I can't right the wrongs done to you, I can say with full conviction that you are a beacon of integrity and my hero. I am so proud of the man I married, a loving husband and father who is an example to our sons. Your joyful outlook is a gift to our family and to all those your life has touched. Thank you for always seeing the glass half full when I couldn't even find the glass. You are my love and best friend.*

# Endnotes

**Introduction**
1. *The United Methodist Hymnal: Book of United Methodist Worship* (Nashville, TN: The United Methodist Publishing House, 1989), 34.
2. Ibid.

**Chapter 2**
1. Eugene Peterson, *The Message* (Colorado Springs, CO: NavPress, 2002), 1937.
2. *Life Application Bible, NIV* (Wheaton, IL: Tyndale House Publishers, Inc. and Grand Rapids, MI: Zondervan Publishing House, 1991), 2270.
3. Mary Demuth, *Beautiful Battle* (Eugene, OR: Harvest House Publishers, 2012), 53.

**Chapter 3**
1. Sylvia Gunter and Arthur Burk, *Blessing Your Spirit: With the Blessings of Your Father and the Names of God* (Birmingham, AL: The Father's Business, 2008), 50.

**Chapter 4**
1. Oswald Chambers, *My Utmost for His Highest* (Grand Rapids, MI: Discovery House Publishers, 1992), November 11.
2. DeMuth, 130.
3. Marjorie Thompson, *Soul Feast* (Louisville, KY: Westminster John Knox Press, 2005), 42, 43.
4. Andrew Murray, *The Ministry of Intercession* (New Kensington, PA: Whitaker House, 1982), 39.

**Chapter 5**
1. Thomas O. Chisolm (words), William M. Runyan (music), 1923, *The United Methodist Hymnal: Book of United Methodist Worship* (Nashville, TN: The United Methodist Publishing House, 1989), 140.
2. Dale Sides, *Mending Cracks in the Soul* (Bedford, VA: Liberating Publications, Inc., 2002), 74.

**Chapter 6**

1. *Life Application Bible, NIV,* 1014, 1015.
2. Edward Mote, *My Hope Is Built, 1834, The United Methodist Hymnal: Book of United Methodist Worship* (Nashville, TN: The United Methodist Publishing House, 1989), 368.
3. Sarah Young, *Jesus Today: Experiencing Hope Through His Presence* (Nashville, TN: Thomas Nelson, 2012), 192.
4. Eric Metaxas, *Miracles: What They Are, Why They Happen, and How They Can Change Your Life* (New York, NY: Penguin Group, 2014), 91.

**Chapter 7**

1. Gunter and Burke, 150.
2. E.M. Bounds, *The Complete Works of E. M. Bounds on Prayer: Experience the Wonders of God Through Prayer* (Grand Rapids, MI: Baker Books, 2004), 45.

**Chapter 8**

1. Dr. Dan B. Allender and Dr. Tremper Longman III, *Cry of the Soul: How Our Emotions Reveal Our Deepest Questions about God* (Colorado Springs, CO: Navpress, 1994), 99.

**Chapter 9**

1. *Life Application Bible, NIV,* 1892.
2. Max Lucado, *You'll Get Through This: Hope and Help for Your Turbulent Times* (Nashville, TN: Thomas Nelson, 2013), 83.
3. Ibid. 84.
4. DeMuth, 216.

**Chapter 10**

1. Mark Buchanan, *Your God Is Too Safe: Rediscovering the Wonder of a God You Can't Control* (Grand Rapids, MI: Multnomah Books, 2001), 220, 221, 228.
2. Bounds, 56.
3. Sylvia Gunter, *You Are Blessed in the Names of God* (Birmingham, AL: The Father's Business, 2008), 137.
4. Ben Patterson, *God's Prayer Book: The Power and Pleasure of Praying the Psalms* (Carol Stream, IL: Tyndale House Publishers, Inc., 2008), 60, 61.
5. Ibid. 83, 84.

## Chapter 11
1. Patterson, 232.
2. Ibid. 93.
3. Bounds, 62.

## Chapter 12
1. Sylvia Gunter, *Prayer Portions* (Birmingham, AL: The Father's Business, 1995), 184.
2. Paula D'Arcy, *Gift of the Red Bird: A Spiritual Encounter* (New York, NY: The Crossroad Publishing Company, 1996), 133, 134.

## Chapter 13
1. Michael Wells, *Problems, God's Presence, and Prayer: Experience the Joy of a Successful Christian Life* (Littleton, CO: Abiding Life Press, 1993), 66.
2. Larry Poland, *The Miracle Walk: A Step-by-Step Journey Through the Supernatural* (Tucson, AZ: Entrust Source Publishers, 2012), 41.
3. John Piper, *Desiring God: Meditations of a Christian Hedonist* (New York, NY: WaterBrook Multnomah Publishers, Inc., 2010), 269, 270.
4. Elizabeth Sherrill, *101 Moments of Prayer: Inspiring Thoughts for Listening to God* (New York, NY: Guideposts, 2014), 70.
5. Demuth, 62.

## Chapter 14
1. Robert J. Morgan, *Red Sea Rules: Ten God-Given Strategies for Difficult Times* (Nashville, TN: Thomas Nelson, 2014), xi, xii.
2. Ibid. 59, 60.
3. *Life Application Bible, NIV*, 682.
4. Philip Yancey, *Our Daily Bread* (Grand Rapids, MI: Our Daily Bread Ministries, 2015), August 5.

## Chapter 15
1. Randy Alcorn, *The Goodness of God: Assurance of Purpose in the Midst of Suffering* (Colorado Springs, CO: Multnomah Books, 2010), 61.
2. Ibid. 47.

## Chapter 16
1. Alcorn, 110.
2. *Life Application Bible, NIV*, 1594.

**Chapter 17**

1. Tim Keller with Kathy Keller, *The Songs of Jesus: A Year of Daily Devotions in the Psalms* (New York, NY: Penguin Random House LLC, 2015), 17.
2. Ibid. 19.
3. Ibid. 51.
4. Ibid. 41.

**Chapter 18**

1. Keller, 119.
2. Peterson, 1071.
3. Ibid. 1082.
4. *Life Application Bible, NIV,* 1555.

**Chapter 19**

1. Keller, 313.
2. Max Lucado, sermon, Oak Hills Church (San Antonio, TX), November 20, 2016.

**Chapter 20**

1. John Bloom, *Things Not Seen: A Fresh Look at Old Stories of Trusting God's Promises* (Wheaton IL: Crossway, 2015), 18, 177.

# Scripture References

| Bible Book | Reference | Chapter in *Signs of His Presence* |
|---|---|---|
| Genesis | 3:15 | 4 |
| | 50:20 | 6 |
| Exodus | 33:14 | 8 |
| | 14:13, 14 | 10, 17 |
| | 15:1, 2, 11, 13 | 11, 14 |
| | 3:11 | 17 |
| | 4:1 | 17 |
| | 5:23 | 17 |
| Leviticus | 16:22 | 10 |
| Numbers | 20:11 | 5 |
| Deuteronomy | 31:8 | 4 |
| | 1:17, 30 | 18 |
| | 31:6 | 18 |
| Judges | 6:23, 24 | 6 |
| | 6:12, 13 | 6 |
| 1 Samuel | 7:12 | 9 |
| | 24:4, 26:7 | 15 |
| 2 Samuel | 22:2, 3 | 2 |
| | 22:1, 2 | 11 |
| | 23:9, 10 | 14 |
| 1 Kings | 19:4 | 14 |
| | 19:11, 12 | 14 |
| 2 Kings | 25:27-29 | 12 |
| | 19:1, 9-16, 19 | 18 |

| Bible Book | Reference | Chapter in *Signs of His Presence* |
|---|---|---|
| 1 Chronicles | 11:12-14 | 14 |
| 2 Chronicles | 20:15 | 2 |
| Job | 19:25 | 3 |
| | 13:15, 16 | 6 |
| Psalms | 46:1 | Foreword |
| | 34:18 | Foreword |
| | 96:3 | Introduction |
| | 91:14, 15 | Introduction |
| | 125:2 | 1 |
| | 91:5 | 2 |
| | 27:8 | 2 |
| | 23:4 | 3 |
| | 91:1 | 3 |
| | 50:15 | 5 |
| | 46:10 | 5 |
| | 13:1-6 | 5 |
| | 22:12-14, 21 | 5 |
| | 35:1-9 | 5 |
| | 63:6, 7 | 5 |
| | 74:15 | 5 |
| | 78:15, 16 | 5 |
| | 105:41 | 5 |
| | 102:6, 7 | 6 |
| | 91:13-15 | 6 |
| | 42:5 | 6 |
| | 69:3, 4 | 6 |
| | 18:2 | 8 |
| | 23:3 | 8 |
| | 31:7 | 8 |
| | 105:39-41 | 9 |
| | 107:35 | 10 |
| | 84:6 | 10 |
| | 27:3, 5 | 11 |
| | 27:13, 14 | 11 |
| | 31:4, 5 | 11 |
| | 42:8 | 13 |
| | 18:2 | 13 |
| | 6:3, 6 | 14 |
| | 13:2 | 14 |
| | 7:9 | 14 |

| Bible Book | Reference | Chapter in *Signs of His Presence* |
|---|---|---|
| Psalms | 8:2 | 15 |
| | 3:3 | 15 |
| | 4:8 | 15 |
| | 9:9 | 15 |
| | 91:13-15 | 15 |
| | 23:5 | 15 |
| | 62:8 | 16 |
| | 55:17 | 16 |
| | 16:7 | 17 |
| | 119:49, 50 | 17 |
| | 56:3 | 18 |
| | 23:2 | 18 |
| | 32:7 | 18 |
| | 42:8 | 18 |
| | Ch. 123 | 18 |
| | Ch. 140 | 18 |
| | 91:1 | 19 |
| | 30:11, 12 | 20 |
| | 23:1-3 | 20 |
| | | |
| Proverbs | 13:12 | 15 |
| | | |
| Ecclesiastes | 3:4 | 4 |
| | 3:16 | 5 |
| | 8:6 | 9 |
| | 12:14 | 15 |
| | | |
| Isaiah | 26:3 | 4 |
| | 50:7 | 5 |
| | 43:20 | 5 |
| | 41:17, 18 | 5 |
| | 48:21 | 5 |
| | 61:3 | 8 |
| | 43:19 | 9 |
| | 8:12-14, 16 | 10 |
| | 53:5 | 13 |
| | 30:32 | 13 |
| | 48:10 | 14 |
| | | |
| Jeremiah | 31:3, 4 | 4 |
| | 31:25 | 7, 18 |
| | 52:31-34 | 12 |

| Bible Book | Reference | Chapter in *Signs of His Presence* |
| --- | --- | --- |
| Jeremiah | 29:11 | 19 |
| | 31:4 | 20 |
| Lamentations | 3:23 | 20 |
| Daniel | 10:12, 13 | 5 |
| | 10:16-18 | 7 |
| Obadiah | 3:18 | 18 |
| Micah | 3:1, 2 | 12 |
| | 5:5 | 12 |
| Nahum | 1:7 | 16 |
| Habakkuk | 3:2 | 6 |
| | 1:3, 4 | 9 |
| | 2:3 | 9 |
| | 3:1 | 15 |
| Matthew | 5:44 | 5 |
| | 25:21 | 7 |
| | 1:23 | 12 |
| | 5:10 | 14 |
| | 5:44, 45 | 17 |
| Mark | 9:24 | 5 |
| Luke | 22:42 | 8 |
| | 10:18 | 15 |
| John | Ch. 9 | 2 |
| | 19:6 | 3 |
| | 15:4 | 6 |
| | 11:4 | 6 |
| | 7:50, 51 | 9 |
| | 9:3 | 9 |
| | 7:51 | 20 |
| Acts | 17:28 | Foreword |
| | 13:6-10 | 2 |
| | 20:24 | 19 |

| Bible Book | Reference | Chapter in *Signs of His Presence* |
|---|---|---|
| Romans | 16:20 | 5 |
| | 12:19, 20 | 8 |
| | 5:3-5 | 17, 20 |
| 1 Corinthians | 10:4 | 10 |
| 2 Corinthians | 10:5 | 4 |
| | 10:4 | 14 |
| | 4:8, 9 | 14 |
| | 1:8, 9 | 15 |
| Ephesians | 6:12 | Introduction, 5 |
| | 4:31 | 12 |
| | 6:11 | 13 |
| Colossians | 1:17 | 17 |
| 1 Thessalonians | 5:16-18 | 12 |
| 2 Timothy | 4:18 | 2 |
| | 1:7 | 18 |
| Hebrews | 6:19, 20 | 6 |
| James | 1:12 | 3 |
| | 1:19 | 3 |
| | 3:13 | 3 |
| 1 Peter | 5:10 | Foreword |
| | 4:12, 13 | 7 |
| | 2:19 | 7 |
| | 3:15 | 20 |
| 2 Peter | 2:11 | 2 |
| | 3:9 | 10 |
| 1 John | 3:8 | Introduction, 2 |
| | 4:4 | 2 |
| | 2:14 | 20 |

# Suggested Books

Alcorn, Randy
*The Goodness of God*

Allender, Dr. Dan B., and Longman III, Dr. Tremper
*The Cry of the Soul*

Bloom, Jon
*Things Not Seen*

Bounds, E.M.
*Guide to Spiritual Warfare*
*Prayer and Spiritual Warfare*
*The Necessity of Prayer*

Buchanan, Mark
*The Rest of God*
*Your God Is Too Safe*

Burk, Arthur, and Gunter, Sylvia
*Blessing Your Spirit*

Cahn, Jonathan
*The Book of Mysteries*

Chambers, Oswald
*My Utmost for His Highest*

Chandler, Matt
*The Explicit Gospel*

D'Arcy, Paula
*Gift of the Red Bird*

DeMuth, Mary
*Beautiful Battle*
*Everything*

Foster, Richard
*Celebration of Discipline*
*Prayer*

Gunter, Sylvia
*You Are Blessed in the Names of God*

Hays, Tommy
*Free to Be Like Jesus*

Heald, Cynthia
*Intimacy with God through the Psalms*

Howard, Betsy Childs
*Seasons of Waiting*

Keller, Timothy, with Keller, Kathy
*The Songs of Jesus*

Lewis, C. S.
*A Grief Observed*
*The Screwtape Letters*

Lucado, Max
*More to Your Story*
*Traveling Light*
*You'll Get Through This*

Metaxas, Eric
*Miracles*

Morgan, Robert J.
*The Red Sea Rules*

Murray, Andrew
*Abide in Christ*
*Experiencing the Holy Spirit*
*The Ministry of Intercession*
*Waiting on God*
*With Christ in the School of Prayer*

Patterson, Ben
*God's Prayer Book*

Peterson, Eugene
   *The Message*

Piper, John
   *Desiring God*

Poland, Larry
   *Miracle Walk*

Ruth, Peggy Joyce
   *Psalm 91*

Shirer, Priscilla
   *Awaken*

Sides, Dale
   *Mending Cracks in the Soul*

Sittser, Gerald Lawson
   *A Grief Disguised*

Spangler, Ann
   *Praying the Names of God*

Thompson, Marjorie J.
   *Soul Feast*

Tozer, A. W.
   *The Pursuit of God*

Voskamp, Ann
   *One Thousand Gifts*

Wells, Michael
   *Problems, God's Presence, and Prayer*

Yancey, Philip
   *Prayer*

Zempel, Heather
   *Amazed and Confused*